Up the EDP Pyramid

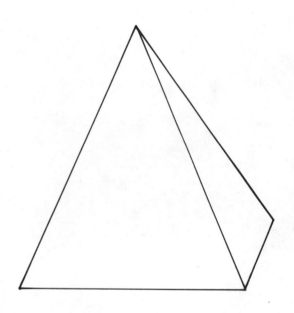

Up the EDP Pyramid

The Complete Job Hunting Manual
for Computer Professionals

JACK FRENCH

A WILEY-INTERSCIENCE PUBLICATION

JOHN WILEY & SONS
New York • Chichester • Brisbane • Toronto • Singapore

This publication is designed to provide accurate and
authoritative information in regard to the subject
matter covered. It is sold with the understanding that
the publisher is not engaged in rendering legal, accounting,
or other professional service. If legal advice or other
expert assistance is required, the services of a competent
professional person should be sought. *From a Declaration
of Principles jointly adopted by a Committee of the
American Bar Association and a Committee of Publishers.*

Library of Congress Cataloging in Publication Data:

French, Jack, 1932-
  Up the EDP Pyramid.

  "A Wiley-Interscience publication."
  Includes index.
  1. Electronic data processing—Vocational guidance. 2. Computers—Vocational guidance.
I. Title.

QA76.25.F73   001.64'023   81-11605
ISBN 0-471-87117-6

Printed in the United States of America

10 9 8 7 6 5 4 3 2 1

*To Cindy, Mark, and Simone
and our short time together . . .
and
To Helen and Troy, wherever you are*

Preface

You may wonder how a book like this came to be. After many years of implementing Data Processing projects, I finally paused for a moment to consider what I had really done that was worth mentioning. I remembered all of the programs, projects, computers, and the late and long hours I had given to this profession. Most of all, I thought of the many fine computer people who became lifelong friends, and of some of those I lost touch with.

Most of the pioneers did not know what would happen in computer technology. Consequently, each job was taken up on the basis of what seemed to be the best thing at the time. Few understood the consequences of their actions or their own capabilities. The latest technology was frequently the master determinate of the next job step. Most pioneers became moderately successful. All would probably agree that things could have been better if they had known then what they know now. They would have planned their careers differently.

While it is not possible to cram experience into the minds of new generations, this book is an attempt to reveal some of the factors the DP professional will face in the course of a data processing career.

Clearly, the United States could not function today without its computers, nor, more important, without its computer people, who perceive and create the computer systems that are behind most scenes of everyday life. Many computer professionals are thoroughly misunderstood by those not involved with the intricacies of automation. Don't let this bother you. It is hoped that this book will give you insights into how to plan your career, deal with the human equations, and get better jobs.

I express my sincere appreciation to Gerry Gilberg and Frank Evans, of Robert Half of Cincinnati, Inc., who struggled so valiantly to teach me what really counts in getting the best jobs for computer professionals; and, of course, to my client companies and candidates who testify daily to the excitement of what is going on in the real world of data processing.

JACK FRENCH

Cincinnati, Ohio
September 1981

Contents

Up the EDP Pyramid

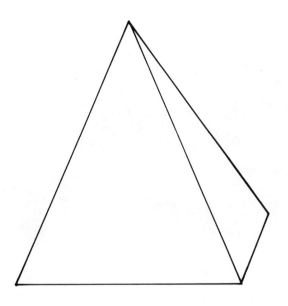

One

Plan Your Data Processing Career

A DEDICATION

This book is dedicated to the business data processing (DP) professionals who are changing America by means of the most significant new industry of our time. Since 1960, the DP industry has encompassed the lives of millions who have contributed their time and life energy to exploit computer technology, to provide companies with increased profits, and to generate a better way of life for all of us.

Often obscured by company images and exploitation, the DP professional can be compared to the miners of the early 1900s. Without a union or a Mother Jones, educated data processors have been left on their own frontier to procure good positions and increased income. In many cases, DP people have been able to achieve a good standard of living, but they have in general received only a small part of the results of their efforts. The demand for computer talent already far exceeds the supply. During the 1980s, the supply will fall short of the demand. Salary levels will increase significantly despite schools' and manufacturers' training programs, intended to meet industrial needs.

PROFESSIONAL LOYALTY

In general, companies have failed to recognize the true value of investment in the DP specialist. In fact, some company tactics actually prohibit free bidding for people possessing valuable DP skills. Consequently, the DP person has developed professional loyalty rather than company loyalty. Data processing activities have more frequently been organized on the basis of service centers to companies, rather than as integral parts of business operations. Because of the specialized training required for DP persons, some companies regard DP staff as mere technicians with little talent or

potential for promotion up into other parts of the business. While accountants, salespeople, and engineers move to the leadership positions, DP professionals are often relegated to supporting roles.

This book is meant to help you plan and develop your DP career to the
maximum of your capability. Unfortunately, you have not had time or the
experience necessary to understand the job improvement process or the
technique of exploiting your own abilities. Years of training, study, and
work experience leave little time to learn and plan the system of raising
your responsibility and income levels to the maximum and at the right time.

In twenty years of directing major computer systems and programming
developments, I have held top jobs with national companies. I have seen
individual successes and failures, well-managed projects, good operations,
and management banzai charges, in which careers were crushed and individuals destroyed.

Every week, I get calls from companies wanting to hire the best DP professionals. Some of these companies understand the value of top-grade
performers. To fill the need, DP personnel leave one company and join
another, looking for a better opportunity to accelerate their career. You
may leave a good company to work for a worse one, because you do not
understand job evaluation in terms of a career plan. You may just sit and
wait, hoping you will be chosen for a better position or higher pay. You
may find that your work is recognized only when you have accepted another offer. You may even succumb to the ever fatal counteroffer. Career
problems are sometimes perceived where none exist; solutions may be perceived to nonproblems, and frequently the wrong solution is applied to the
real problem. You yourself may be the real problem.

Some of the following circumstances may cause you to think of
changing jobs.

Your salary is not competitive with that of other DP professionals of equivalent experience.

Your overtime is taken for granted.

You have been passed over for advancement. New bosses appear in positions for which you qualify.

Your work gets little recognition.

Your boss will not recommend you for a higher position or experience-
enhancing assignments.

There are no positions into which you can advance.

Promises are not kept.

There is no means to keep up with the state of the art in hardware or software.

Management politics are too thick.

Staff turnover exists due to poor administration.

Company fringe benefits are low.

Your job simply isn't enjoyable any more.

Before you make any irrational decisions, you should understand why some professionals move up and why others just move. The reason data processors move frequently to achieve advancement has to do with the life cycle of a specific system, and their career timing. The activity of creating and installing a new system is worth a major company investment, but once the system is installed, the maintenance function is thought to be worth considerably less. Remember, there are no permanent jobs in data processing. The day of the gold watch is over.

THE CHALLENGE

The forecast for the DP job market in the next decade is excellent for all classes and levels of DP specialists. Catch-22 is that premium DP jobs, those offering the best opportunities for continuing education, personal satisfaction, and advancement will still be difficult to identify and obtain in your career schedule. The competition will be hot and heavy. Like the Boston Marathon, many will start, but many will collapse when they meet the competition. Fewer will stretch out ahead of the pack, and only the best will achieve number one positions in their pyramid.

There are few shortcuts. If you could see the rough terrain ahead, you might even choose another field for a career. Many DP pyramid heads today are not sure how they reached their position. Some do not even deserve their title and have retired on the job. In some situations, their bosses are not yet fully conversant with DP technology and are reluctant to make a change. This situation is altering quickly, however, owing to the high cost of hard-to-find DP professionals. In DP there can be no retirement. You either progress up or out. The new breed of computer professional will force companies to maintain only the best at the top of the pyramid, or else everyone will leave and no one will join.

Electronic data processing (EDP) turnover is expected to go above 60 percent annually for college-educated personnel. Companies still can't seem to understand the uniqueness of today's DP specialists. Few will understand your addiction to your field except other addicts. To be good at what you do in computers requires addiction. It has a psychology all of its own, tied to our times. What it will do to you is your choice. Long hours, isolation, discipline, frustration, and pressure can leave their mark on your personality. Properly conditioned DP professionals need not accept their profession as part of the age of indifference.

The power of the computer is only in its infancy. The sophisticated devices and software of 2001 will make today's hardware and software look like Model T Fords. It is no secret that the industrial age is giving way to the computer age in ways no one imagined even twenty years ago. Your importance to the creativity of our times over the next twenty years cannot be overestimated. Your contribution to our civilization will demand as much time and work as any other professional who influences history. Computer specialists are frequently akin to artists, musicians, writers, and other researchers who effect change in civilization. Your perception of what you are doing at every point in your career makes the difference.

In the political world, metamorphosis starts with people of words and ideas, followed by revolutionary fanatics, who finally succumb to the administrators. Then the cycle begins again. So it is in the cycle of computer systems. New computerization is conceived and planned, followed by implementation/conversion, which finally turns into maintenance—until the planners commence the cycle once again. Careers are enhanced when DP people ride the crest and don't get caught in the trough.

Many words have been written about how to get interviews, offers, and jobs. This book is addressed expressly to the EDP professional and concerns the many factors that directly affect recruiting, hiring, and promotion to key positions. Your job will occupy a large portion of your life. It is fundamental to your psychological and mental well-being to enjoy it and understand it. The DP profession is not for everyone just because it pays well. The profession may at first glance appear narrow, but on further examination, you can see that the span of talents required includes many disciplines and broad general knowledge. It will strain your capacity to learn and drain your emotions at times. Computerland is not for the weak or narrow-minded. The major systems are a strange blend of human interaction and programmed response. You are the renaissance men and women of the future.

It is hoped that this book will give you insight into your career. Job hunting for the sake of another dollar is not purposeful. Job hunting for a totally satisfactory and broad career is the purpose. Realism and humor must prevail. Your career is a struggle at best, but you might as well know up front what to expect. The agony of defeat and the ecstacy of accomplishment are both there, in spite of your best-laid plans. Frequently, your ability to do a job has almost nothing to do with your ability to get hired, but the results of this fact can be humiliating.

The full scope of your career involves several factors. Depending on where you are in your career, each of the following factors will affect your judgment of what is best for you. This book is organized around these factors of DP job selection.

Your Objectives and Goals

Location of the job
The industry

The companies within the industry
The job class and level of experience
Business applications
System activities
Technical activities
Technical functions
Computer hardware and software
The boss
The pay scales

If you are successful, you will hold many positions in your DP career. Each will be evaluated on its own merits in your climb up the pyramid. Every time you change jobs, you will sell the skills you have acquired previously, but you must also acquire new skills to trade in the future for the next job. It is an iterative process, a metamorphosis, and you have to avoid getting in a loop.

You may first want to scan this book quickly for its organization and reference, then go into detail. Definitions are important, and some time is spent on the meanings of words, to avoid confusion.

ACTION REQUIRED

If you value your career, you must plan it as diligently as you perform your day-to-day job. You must be ever vigilant for opportunities for advancement at the beginning of new system developments. You must analyze bad job situations where no advancement is possible. You must continually improve your own competence and skills in many business areas. Data processing must and will support business activities, not vice versa.

The rest of this book is about improving your DP career. It is a guideline for your planning and should provide a systematic approach. It is not a cookbook of recipes for explicit results. Only you can write that book in your lifetime in data processing. You must continuously prepare yourself to get the best jobs. I assume you want it straight, so here it is. Remember Crane's Law: There is no such thing as a free lunch.

All experience hath shown that mankind are more disposed to suffer, while evils are sufferable, than to right themselves by abolishing the forms to which they are accustomed.

Declaration of Independence
July 4, 1776

Two

Know the Organization
of Your Company

THE BUSINESS HIERARCHY

The business hierarchy of a typical company is displayed in Figure 2-1. It is essential that you understand the typical business hierarchy and its terminology, so that any position in your DP career within a company can be accurately evaluated. The business pyramid establishes an overview so that your DP career potential can be properly appraised relative to companies and jobs. Your detail resume should be created and maintained using common business terminology. You will then be better able to discuss your background with prospective employers and achieve responsible positions more quickly.

Clearly, data processing supports the pyramid of most major companies. It is important that you appreciate how DP functions support all aspects of your company's business. The following section starts at the top of the business pyramid and describes the various levels of management. The definitions and terminology used should be helpful in placing your DP career from the perspective of business operations.

Company Objectives and Goals

Senior management establishes company objectives and goals. Policies are established to provide rules that guide company personnel in attaining objectives and meeting goals. Strategic planning is necessary to ensure that the objectives and goals are right for the company.

Business objectives are usually expressed as strategic statements of long-term purpose in terms of the followng.

Enduring, timeless, and continuing guidelines
Strategic and policy decisions
Company products, services, reliability, prices, and profits

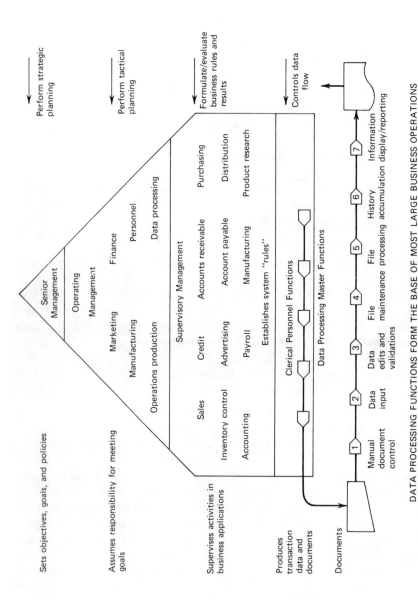

DATA PROCESSING FUNCTIONS FORM THE BASE OF MOST LARGE BUSINESS OPERATIONS

Figure 2-1 The business hierarchy.

7

Examples of typical business objectives are:

To increase business profits
To maximize return on invested capital
To outperform competitors
To achieve growth in sales and physical sites
To increase productivity
To control complexity
To provide quality products and services
To maintain and support highly competent management

Examples of some well-known slogans depicting these objectives are:

"Service is our most important product"
"Serving America through research"
"Better life through electricity"
"Your protection is our business"
"The system is the solution"

Business goals supplement company objectives. Goals differ from objectives and are expressed as specific (one-time) targets for planning and tactical action by operating management, attainable within a given time-frame, usually a year. Examples of business goals are:

To introduce product X by August of this year
To increase sales by 9 percent this year
To decrease payroll expense by 4 percent this year
To install a new order entry system in nine months
To install 30 percent more computer capability by year's end

Business goals are usually the result of the joint planning efforts of senior and operating management. Knowledge of major goals is important to you in order to ensure that your prime assignments relate directly to those goals. If you don't know the goals, you may find yourself maintaining the old systems, limiting your management exposure, and losing out on assignments that could significantly advance your career.

Company objectives usually change slowly and require some significant long-range planning to identify. Company goals to meet those objectives may be adjusted quickly as a result of economic conditions, available resources, consumer needs, available technology, or governmental actions.

Examples of objective and goal changes can be found in the effects on oil companies of the recent shortage of crude oil. The chain effect can be observed in auto companies in the rush to provide more economical automobiles. Changes in computer technology have provided lower hardware costs, and consequently, the minicomputer appeared, making computers available for more and smaller companies. Obsolescence takes its toll. Technology makes it possible to introduce more labor-saving devices but often requires more technically qualified personnel to build and operate the new robots of our time. Remember that through it all: "Systems change, but instincts remain."

The last wave has not yet come in. In fact, the major storms are just on the horizon in the so-called free-enterprise system. Change is what we can count on.

Product planning and development time actually can take longer than the useful life of the product itself. Computer systems are no exception to this phenomenon. No sooner is the new business support system installed than it is unable to meet the ever changing needs of the business. The development cycle begins again and again.

If you are not vitally interested in these exciting events as they relate to your company's products you probably are not going to go too far in your EDP career.

Responsibility Centers and Organization

Responsibilities are assigned to operating management within a company and determine the structure of the company organization to meet objectives and establish goals. Typical responsibility centers are:

Marketing	Finance/accounting
Manufacturing	Administration
Engineering	Research
Operations/Production	Personnel
Distribution	Data Processing

"Responsibility" can be interpreted as financial, mental, legal, and moral commitments for meeting objectives and accomplishing goals. One of the major responsibility centers in a company is frequently the DP department. The pyramid head of DP is responsible for all the DP activities and functions. Many DP professionals do not comprehend the magnitude of the responsibilities of the head of data procesing. The managerial skills required to manage and direct a complex DP installation are far different from those required to code programs and operate computers. It is clear that many technical computer personnel will never acquire the management skills to lead a major DP organization. If you aspire to reach the top of the EDP pyramid, your career must be directed early toward multiple job classifications and higher job levels. Some companies may initially hire a technician to manage data processing but in time will turn to the professional manager who has supplemented his technical career with education and activities that span the other responsibility areas of the company.

The responsibility centers of the company frequently are the foundation of the company revenue and cost center numbering system. These numbers identify where the company events occur and, consequently, who is responsible. You should learn your company's numbering system so that you can readily use it in your DP activity. Company accounts describe what has happened and center numbers describe where. If you would learn about your company, the first and foremost system in which to gain experience is the general ledger. All other EDP systems eventually interface with the general ledger system. No DP professional is complete without this experience. If you majored in accounting, you probably are a big step ahead of your competition in business data processing.

Responsibilities require dedicated people who constantly perceive what is needed to improve operations, to plan necessary changes, and to plan how changes should be scheduled and implemented.

In the past, parts of the business could be automated piecemeal, provided proper attention was paid to the interfaces between the parts. As all business components become semiautomated, the economics of future full-scale integration become clear, but the activity of such integration can become too complex to accomplish in one project. The people problem becomes enormous. The responsibility of computer support system planning thus becomes more complex and important than running the current computer operation and requires different perceptual and intuitive skills than those of the (master mechanic) computer programmer.

The responsibility of system change is sometimes compared to changing jet engines in midair. It is frequently better to build a new plane and replace the present fleet than to modify each of the operating components. Many large companies have formed a new responsibility center concentrating solely on computer support planning for all of the other responsibility centers. Separate groups have been formed to create the new systems. Great computerized advances come more often from replacing systems entirely than from modifying current systems.

Clearly, responsibility centers add to or deplete the revenue of the company. Data processing must help to provide information for the revenue centers and reduce operating costs of the expense centers.

Management Activities and Business Applications

Supervisory management activities are organized under the major responsibility centers of the company. Supervisory staffs perform the following activities:

Interpreting information

Formulating plans and budgets

Establishing definitions, procedures, and functions

Prescribing the rules of the system

Determining information needs

Providing employee direction and training

Establishing measures of performance

Monitoring employee and computerized functions

Interacting with customers and vendors

These activities support business applications such as those named in Table 2-1.

To fully enhance your DP career, you should quickly gain experience in all of the major business applications of your company. Many companies have the basic business applications and many specialized applications. The more business applications you know, the greater DP responsibility you can assume.

Table 2-1   Common business application names

Accounting (general, cost, trust, loan, governmental	Inventory Control
Accounts payable	Job cost control
Accounts receivable	Operations research
Billing	Manufacturing control (shop floor)
Bill of material	Merchandising
Brokerage	Numerical control
Credit	Payroll
Demand deposits (banking)	Personnel
Direct mail	Production scheduling
Expense payables	Process control
Financial analysis	Purchasing/receiving
Freight control	Sales analysis
General ledger	Sales control (point of sale)
Insurance (health, life, auto, casulty)	Warehousing

Probably no DP book could be considered complete without an explanation of systems. The business applications in Table 2-1 are a group of related functions, which together form the total system of the company. You can distinguish between the structure of the system and how it functions, but they are always likely to be discussed together.

Data processing has developed over the years initially by simply automating what was currently being done by human hands in a few areas. The structure of human work was frequently sequential and the system structure (or architecture) was modified to fit what seemed to be the best process of doing things. In data processing this sequential process is referred to as batch mode. In other words, the process created the structure.

In the future, it appears that the structure may in fact govern the process. New computer technology enables the speed of feedback to direct, control, and facilite human action, rather than to depend on it. This structure is referred to as on-line real time, where many processes occur simultaneously, relying on common rules and data called data bases.

By learning the business applications of your company and their supporting systems of forms, procedures, and rules, you can understand the advantages of integrated systems. Without detailed knowledge, you will end up recreating the same system. Planning expertise, geared to company objectives, is critical to your long-range career in business data processing. The complexity of this effort is no small matter.

Some distinction should be drawn between data and information. Data are sets of like factors such as names, locations, or items. Information is a collection of data sets put together so that they have relational meaning for planning and control activity. Building a system to create information is one activity. Interpreting the information for decision making is another activity. Typically, DP careers have covered only the creation of information. Future DP careers will require a much fuller understanding of information usage across many business applications.

Consistency in information from one business application area to another is an important factor in DP progress. Common perception of the same information and data to be used by personnel in all areas of the company will be enhanced by the data base technologies of the future.

Rules of Business Applications

All business applications have rules, frequently established by supervisory management. These rules are the basis of computer programs and information reporting. Data processing professionals must always work closely with supervisory management to ensure that the correct data are captured, controlled, programmed, processed, and reported in compliance with the rules of the company. Some examples of business application rules are:

1 Maintain and display sales dollars by product class, by week, this year and last year.

2 Maintain product inventory using last-in, first-out (LIFO) method of inventory evaluation.

3 Bill customers monthly with 10-day allowance for payment, adding a 5 percent service charge monthly on late pay balances.

4 Produce purchase orders and corresponding receiving documents daily.

5 Apply all possible discounts to vendor invoices regardless of the vendor invoice amount or date.

6 Use only six standard payroll job classifications.

7 Post journal entries to the general ledger on the basis of transaction date, not processing date.

8 Pay vendors for only the product quantity invoiced, even if a greater quantity was received.

9 Pay the invoiced item amount, when it is less than the purchase contract amount, but not if it is more than the purchase order amount.

Some of DP program rules may give the DP staff an ethics dilemma. It is clear that the DP professional who understands the rules of company business applications, how they are changed, and who is responsible for them, also understands the company business. The path to advancement, however, lies in discerning which rules should be substained and which would be changed, and why.

As many programmers have discovered, a single business application rule change can effect hundreds of programs in different systems. Old and new rules can, undetected, exist side by side in different but related systems, usually resulting in much human confusion. Documentation of rules can be a lifetime career in a single company. With many rules locked up in computers, managers are often trapped by the very systems and business applications for which they are responsible. The robot has won again because the whole system gets too complex for any one individual to comprehend, yet alone change in any reasonable manner.

A challenge to future DP professionals is to create software that facilitates putting rule changes into the system, and not that simply executes them faster. The DC-3 may still be better in certain situations than the Concorde jet, because the pilot can more quickly change the rules of the flight plan.

Clerical Functions

Clerical functions are executed by personnel in all business application areas. Functions are a series of repetitive tasks sequentially performed in accordance with established rules. A function can be executed by either a person or a computer. Examples of clerical or manual functions are:

Matching invoices to receipts or purchase orders

Placing merchandise in warehouse locations

Summarizing payroll time cards

Date-stamping sales receipts

Keypunching documents

Converting programs from one computer language to another

Data processing professionals learn clerical business functions so that business application workflows can be made more efficient. When clerical functions can be replaced by computer functions, economies usually result. Systems analysts are usually well aware of the cost of each function in the business application workflow for which they are responsible. Knowledge of these costs enables you to evaluate your contribution and worth to the company when you install a new system. When your DP assignments become purely functional (maintenance), it is time to reevaluate your job and career.

Computer technology has helped to eliminate many clerical functions, but has substituted ever boring computer programming maintenance caused by inefficiently written programs. Few people are able to program efficiently, and so the task of maintaining programs falls on more people. Clearly, computer hacks of the future will labor at many small corrections to errors in programs created by others.

When clerical functions are changed in the course of systems implementation, people frequently rebel. Unperceived problems occur. More systems fail because of people than because of the weakness of the design. New systems are always expanding and encroaching on human functions—the new era is here.

A system attracts systems-type people who can succeed within it as well as those who can feed on or hide behind it. Therefore, you must consider their problems when you prescribe new system functions.

The Data Processing Master Functions

The DP functional stream of any business application area is clearly a continuation of clerical functions. Seven basic master functions exist for all automated business applications.

1   Manual control
    The edit and control of basic business documents (i.e., batch dollars, counts, or document control numbers)
2   Data Input
    Keying or transforming document data elements into computer readable formats or media

3 Computer edits and validation
Computerized checking of data element accuracy or file validity comparisons (on line or batch mode)

4 File updating
Records are added, changed, or deleted from the computer file
Posting transactions to computerized files (records on line or batch mode)

5 File processing
Processing of computerized files, using existing data and a set of programmed *rules* to produce correlations, summarizations, or new combinations of elements for control or human prompting

6 History accumulation
Summarizing and storage of computerized files for future use

7 Data display
Scanning computer files to produce a sequential or summarized set of data, called information
Displaying computer records on line, using an automated terminal

The DP master functions exist with either batch-type or on-line types of computer systems. The master functions are required, whether the files are sequential or structured in a data base format. The functions may be executed simultaneously or sequentially.

What all of this means is that you should begin thinking about what you really want to be doing in your DP career. Perhaps you have been involved with these concepts for a long time. You might then ask yourself, "What did I really do that's worth mentioning? What can I take with me into the future?" Glory buys little and reputations must be continuously refreshed.

The major objectives of DP departments are to collect, store, and correlate data, and to display information. Future objectives include controlling, directing, and assisting human activity and functions. Many DP professionals overlook the seven master functions in bidding for DP assignments. Clearly, file processing assignments yield more experience than data editing assignments. Data display assignments can teach you a great deal about company business, if you learn what the information means and how it is used.

WHY SYSTEMS CHANGE

Basically, manual and computerized systems require change when the following occur:

New products or services are introduced

Business objectives and policies change

New business goals are established

Business application rules are changed

New information correlations are required

The organization and responsibilities change

Locations of the company plant change

Volume requirements exceed the current functional system load capabilities

Functional costs can be minimized using new computer technology, procedures, or file structures (data bases)

These changes can mean increased opportunities for you, the DP professional. You can make rapid career advances by taking advantage of knowledge of what is about to occur within a company.

Frequently, senior management is too far removed from DP activities to realize the effect of their decisions on them. Often, the DP manager is caught up in day-to-day activities and is unable to perceive or to plan new DP techniques to support business changes. When this occurs, the old system is enhanced until it falls under its own weight, sometimes on your career.

Frequently, a system that performs certain functions continues to operate, regardless of changing conditions. Complex systems designed from new requirements never work. You have to start with already working simple systems.

It is important for you to evaluate the senior and DP management of your company, their knowledge of and commitment to DP improvements. Company DP plans and budgets reflect the level of opportunity for career development. Your career advancement will depend on how quickly the company is changing. Where senior management is heavily involved in data processing your career progress is usually good.

The time to get work assignments is before you accept employment and when you know the company goals. After you are hired, it is difficult to negotiate your assignments because of immediate company needs. Few DP professionals question company goals and objectives until late in their career, and then it is often too late.

THE COMPANY

Companies differ significantly in their treatment of the DP function. Data processing is the bread and butter of some companies, since the entire business may hinge on the quality of the DP operation. The best DP positions and opportunities exist in those companies where computer use is part of the "mainstream" of the business. Conversely, in those companies where the computer is only a large accounting or payroll machine, opportunities are almost nonexistent. In evaluating your company you may want to ask the following:

1 Where does the company rank in the industry in terms of sales and profits?
2 What has been company growth in the past three years in terms of sales, profits, and assets?
3 What is the management and employee turnover? It affects your career.
4 How is the data processing department organized and to whom does it report?
5 What significant data systems have been installed in the last two years?
6 What projects are planned for the next two years?
7 Are the DP outlays increasing as a percentage of sales?
8 Where did your predecessor go and why?
9 What is the professional experience of your boss?
10 How many data processors have been promoted to other company positions in the last two years?

The answers to these questions will give you good insights into the company and your chances for advancement in the company pyramid.

It is clear that some companies are young and aggressive and some are old and dying. Some are barely on their feet and are facing bankruptcy, even in good industries. Some companies produce a single product and some are conglomerates. Some are making buggy whips and others are always producing products of the future. Some companies have not yet discovered the computer, while others are highly advanced in computer technology. Some companies have old management waiting for retirement and some have managements as young as you. Some companies are using their computer power only to record what happened yesterday. Other companies are using their computer power to predict and create tomorrow. Some companies are embarked on enormous projects that will take years and may fall of their own weight. Others take a planned, piece-by-piece approach. Others don't know what they are doing. Some companies have jobs that can significantly enhance your career. Others have jobs that pay a fair wage but go nowhere.

Which will you choose? Will you even care if you can make a dollar more and they just happen to have a new computer? Will you do your homework before donating a valuable segment of your career to the company?

THE INDUSTRY

The DP professional often is not aware of the importance of continuing experience in a given industry. A list of industry names may be found in Table 2-2. Your knowledge of an industry is valuable to any employer in that industry because your judgments in your day-to-day work will be more beneficial to the business. Insurance companies prefer DP people who know insurance business applications. Bankers prefer banking application experience, retailers prefer retailing experience, and manufacturers prefer manufacturing experience. Clearly, you should select and stay in an industry in which you can develop a keen interest and knowledge of all phases of its products and operations, not simply DP techniques. Without industry knowledge you may never get a chance for a top DP position. Industry experience may not be a consideration where your technical skills are needed at the moment. If, however, you are in competition with someone with equal skills who has industry-related experience, you lose. There is no substitute for the ability to discuss all aspects of your industry. You may change employers, but try to stay in the same industry or related ones. In the long run you will be able to command a better salary. You can always emphasize your experience in an industry during salary reviews or for job interviews to display your worth to a company.

Table 2-2   Common industry names

Advertising	Consulting	Insurance
Aircraft	Distribution	Manufacturing
Airline	Education	Medical/health care
Automobile	Engineering	Pharmaceutical
Auditing/accounting	Energy	Printing/publishing
Banking/finance	Electronics	Real estate
Brokerage	Farming	Retail
Chemical	Food processing	Scientific
Computer/Software	Grocery	Transportation
Construction	Government	Utilities

Take a moment to review Figure 2-1. The DP function within most companies should be clear. It may give you at least one frame of reference, even if you want to develop others.

At this point, countless examples of computer automation within various industries could be discussed, ranging from airline reservation systems to retail point-of-sale devices, from highly complex factory scheduling systems to numerical control of machines, or from energy control systems to governmental payroll systems. These types of systems can be reviewed by reading *Datamation* magazine, countless papers submitted by systems engineers in respective industries to computer conferences and those described frequently in the weekly publication, *Computerworld*. See if you can discover which industries are most likely to automate the most fully and which companies within those industries will advance the fastest. When you figure it out, please let me know. It is obvious that a few industries have a high concentration of wealth. These industries will invest heavily in new computer technology and software to increase their profits and industry position as EDP planning shows targets of opportunity.

SUMMARY

The aim of this chapter is to help you think of the position of DP activities and functions within companies, which make up different industries.

Create your own company pyramid and then determine how much you know about its organization, objectives, goals, business applications, activities, systems, rules, and functions and why they are changing.

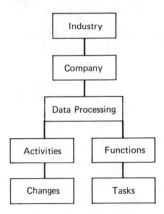

By understanding the position of data processing in the organization of the company of your choice, you are better able to plan your subsequent career moves up the pyramid.

Now you are ready to take a closer look at the actual job components of data processing and think about what experience you really want to get.

Three

Determine What Experience You Need and How to Get It

THE DATA PROCESSING ORGANIZATION OF A LARGE COMPANY

A typical DP organization is displayed in Figure 3-1. There are many variations in DP organizations, depending on company size, sophistication, and assigned responsibilities. The best DP organizations are built on the strengths of staff members. The job levels displayed in Figure 3-1 do not imply equivalent responsibilities or rates of pay. Generally, the systems and programming staff have higher salary levels than the function operations staff. Those DP positions that effect change can be classified as DP activities. Those DP jobs that accomplish repetitive tasks can be classified as DP functions.

The job names in Figure 3-1 are typical of those used in data processing, and there are frequently many individuals in one DP organization with the same job name. It is important for you to know how many persons in your company have the same job as you and what job classes and levels exist, as well as their salary ranges. You should know the background of your competition so that you can gage where you stand in the potential promotion list.

If the DP pyramid head reports directly to the company president, top management is involved. If this person reports to a controller or financial officer, DP functions may merely support bookkeeping functions, rather than being the main product of the company. Where the DP department directly reports to the head of marketing or manufacturing, DP opportunities are usually promising.

Job Classifications and Levels

Table 3-1 displays some common DP job classifications and levels. By coupling the job class with the job level, almost all DP jobs can be ade-

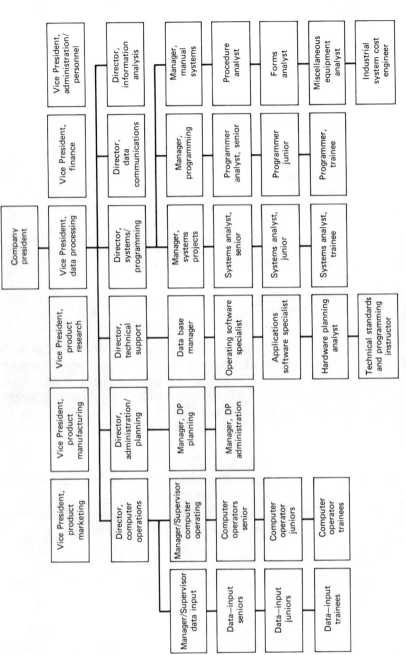

Figure 3-1 The data processing organization of a large company

21

quately named. In your résumé it is important to use common job classes and levels to describe your responsibility. Avoid using names that might be peculiar to a particular company or confuse the reader.

Table 3-1   Common DP job classifications and levels

Job Classifications	Job Levels
Data control	Clerical
Data input	Trainee
Data distribution	Junior
Computer operator	Senior
Systems analyst	Supervisor
Programmer	Project leader
Software systems	Project manager
Data base	Manager
DP planning	Specialist
Consultant	Director
Management science	Vice president
Marketing	
Engineering	
Communication	

This chapter describes activities and functions in which you may be engaged, even though your job name may imply only one type of activity. You may legitimately refer to your work by the appropriate job name, even if you did not actually hold the job title. Consider the following activities you might engage in during your DP career:

1 Acting as a systems analyst, designed a payroll system to pay employees weekly.
2 Acting as a systems programmer, accomplished system generations to allow for a more efficient computer operation.
3 Acting as a programmer analyst, gathered user requirements and wrote program specifications for the accounts payable application.
4 Acting as a data base analyst, designed common files for multiple business applications.
5 Acting as a project leader, directed systems analysts and programmers in implementation of a new manufacturing system.

You should display effectively tasks you have actually accomplished that relate to job names other than the one you have. Experience in multiple job classes and levels is the quickest way up the EDP pyramid. Never allow yourself to use up five years in coding COBOL programs according to specifications written by others.

Technology has created traps of more and more specialities in DP jobs. Frequently, job classes/levels have expanded to limit breadth of knowledge and encapsulate the DP professional in deep, narrow areas. The narrower and deeper you dive, the fewer options you have in your career.

The opportunity to gain experience quickly across multiple job classes and levels is frequently related to the size and policies of the company. Large companies usually have longer experience tenure requirements than smaller companies before a different job class opportunity is presented to an employee, because the costs of cross-training a large staff and job class pay differentials are high. For example, it is unlikely that a senior systems analyst in a large company would be given an opportunity to be the computer operations manager, regardless of the value of horizontal experience in proceeding up the pyramid. A computer room operating shift supervisor would probably have difficulty gaining experience as a systems analyst. A keypunch supervisor might have trouble convincing a large employer to give her a programming opportunity. Vertical progress is more likely in a large company than in a smaller one (see figure 3-1). Some really cheap companies insist that proven employees take a pay cut in return of a so-called opportunity. You may want to take the cut to get horizontal experience and then switch companies. Good companies would sustain your pay rate while cross-training you. Stay with that company; you can move up. Give it all you've got, but insist on training.

Smaller companies can frequently give you a lot of experience in data input, computer room operations, programming, and systems design, simply because budgets require the staff to perform multiple activities. Sometimes the formal training budget will not reimburse you for training or vendor schools when you need it. You should be cautious, however, about being given great responsibility before you have mastered the rudiments of DP. For example, a DP manager ahead of his time may in a smaller company achieve a position and salary level that prohibit him from moving, with the same title, to a larger company. A larger company may prefer to promote from within.

A systems analyst in a larger company may earn more than a DP manager in a smaller company. A DP manager may not want to relinquish his title for a systems analyst position in a larger company, even for a good pay increase. Larger companies at least pay lip service to promotion from within and resist hiring ex–DP managers for lesser-titled positions or narrower responsibilities.

Conversely, a systems analyst in a larger company may find a DP manager job hard to get in a smaller company. Some smaller companies may refuse to hire some well-qualified, large-company DP professionals because they fear that their smaller environment would soon frustrate the fast-track, high-technology individual. The narrow experience of only programming or systems work in a larger company may exclude you from running a computer operation of smaller company.

In summary, the dilemma of progress is established. The DP head must gain experience in management operations, technical, and developmental activities. Clearly, you can find yourself in many career traps if you are on your way to the top of the pyramid. Without a plan you are lost.

Business Applications and Systems Activity

The business applications discussed in Chapter 2 and displayed in Table 2-1 are supported by their respective functional systems. It is clear that the more business application systems you can gain experience in, the more valuable you are to any company.

The DP professional must not forget that advancement depends on much more than knowledge of specific computer hardware and software intricacies. After all, what does it matter what is in the DAT ("Data Translation Hardware") box: tomorrow it will be replaced with new technology.

You can advance your career significantly by engaging in new systems development projects. Common system activities are displayed in Table 3-2.

Table 3-2   Common system activities

Business requirements planning	System user training
System documentation	System control specifications
System design and analysis	System marketing
Data base design	Microfiche microfilm studies
System flowcharting	Computer printing studies
Manual system and procedure design	Computer microfilm studies
System economics analysis	Project control planning (PERT)
Forms design	Information display design
Standard procedure writing	Computer hardware capacity and
Data input formating	performance planning
Base-case formulation and testing	Computer software performance planning
Computer operations instruction	System standards development
System user manual preparation	Long-range system planning

During a systems project you will have an opportunity to engage in many of the activities listed and to learn the rules. The systems activity will give you an opportunity to work with many users within the company. It will allow you to very quickly gain a broad business application knowledge.

Many system users are operations-oriented; they are charged with keeping production flowing under the current system. After your analysis of what users are doing, you will prescribe a new way of performing functions, possibly using the power of the computer with a new set of rules.

Your tendency may be to create an elaborate computerized wrapping complete with bells and whistles. Many system users understand only plain brown wrapping paper. The simpler you can make life, the better you will be remembered, regardless of your creative ability or the fun of programming the world. Programs never work the first time. A simple system works sometimes. Complex programs never work. Tight systems reduce human thinking, and people start to find ways to circumvent the system. New systems always create new problems and needs.

Remember: Keep it simple.

The quicker you are able to implement a better way of doing things in one business application area, the faster you can move on to another area. Management will be impressed only by those who create or modify a system or display information for their operations staff quickly. Long duration, complicated projects seldom if ever progress as originally planned. If you are tied up for a prolonged period of time on a single project or business application, you may not be able to move up in an organization when an opportunity occurs. You won't be any more qualified after four years in accounts payable than at the end of two years. Your career may end because you have become the resident expert in a single business application.

You must be able to demonstrate that you can work with all levels of the operational staff in spite of any incompetence on their part. Failure at this human skill will end your DP career quickly. Operating users will establish your DP professional reputation.

After you have learned the basic business applications, system functions, and rules, you may have the opportunity to confer with senior management. If this occurs, you are on your way up the EDP pyramid. Each higher management level requires simpler and broader presentations than the previous level. One of the major problems caused by operating users is that they try to prescribe not only what they require, but also how the system should function. Sometimes the user's prescription causes the system and programming staff endless sequence and logic problems, together with high ongoing system maintenance costs. Getting tied up over a prolonged period with a system that proves too complex to fly can be a disastrous career setback.

Evolution in small pieces is the key to career success. Sometimes even the smallest of systems results can make you a hero in your own time. Avoid major surgery at all costs and remember Macchiavelli's words in *The Prince* written in 1513:

It must be remembered that there is nothing more difficult to plan, more doubtful of success nor more dangerous to manage than the creation of a new system. For the initiator has the enmity of all who would profit by the preservation of the old institution and merely lukewarm defenders in those who would gain by the new one.

Technical Activities and Functions

A broad base of technical activities is essential for all DP professionals. Table 3-3 is a list of common technical activities. It is important for you in your career to master several technical activities in at least one hardware/ software discipline. You will definitely broaden your career if you also engage in some of the basic DP functions, including the following:

Input/output distribution control

Data-input keying

Word processing

Computer scheduling and production control

Computer job setup and operations

Computer file and systems documentation librarian

Computer technology has never failed to change. As soon as one kind of computer equipment and software is produced, a replacement appears on the horizon. It is virtually impossible to stay on top of all of the new technology as it develops.

The choice between a technical or management DP career must come early. Typically, after the basic skills are mastered, the DP business career offers three choices:

System development

Technical software systems

Computer operations

Clearly, the technically intensive DP professional must keep up to date on new equipment and associated software. If the DP professional plans a management-intensive career, specific hardware/software detail become less important. The typical DP career follows these stages:

1 Programming/Operating
2 Programming analysis
3 Systems analysis

Table 3-3 Common activities and functions

Technical Activities	Technical Functions	Administrative Activities
Technical system design	Input/outout distribution	Budget planning
Program specification	control	Manpower planning
documentation	Data-input keying	Employee recruiting
Software development	Computer and personnel	and hiring
compilers, translators,	scheduling and	Employee performance
interpreters, operating	production control	standards development
systems	Word processing	Performance and salary
Software analysis selec-	Computer operations	reviews
tion and modification	and job setups	Employee salary
Software installation	Tape librarian	administration
System generation	Systems librarian	
(sys gen)	Document control	
Business application		
programming		
Communication software		
programming		
Data-input programming		
Data base technical		
physical design		
Computer cost performance		
measurements		
Programming standards		
development		
Computer facilities planning		
Computer operations planning		
Training technical staff		
Technical consulting		
Computer hardware		
comparison studies		
Computer capacity		
performance measurements		
Computer file utilization		
measurements		
Scientific application		
programming		
Structured programming		
Computer network designs		
Utility programming		
Mathematical modeling		
Data/file backup/security planning		
Linear programming		
Simulation programming		
Operations standards and development		

4   Senior programming analysis

5   Project leader

6   Manager, programming or systems

7   Manager, operations, or manager, technical support software, or manager, planning

8   Directorship or vice presidency

Many have tried to circumvent the detail hardware logic of the beginning steps in the race to the top. After one COBOL program, they claim to be ready to do systems work or be project managers. Technical disciplines are a problem to them and logic detail is not their forte. If they are good talkers and politicians they seem to move quickly. These artists often snow management and can be detrimental to your career. They can promise fast implementations, create rainbows, and talk in circles much faster than you can program and implement.

Do not be in such a big rush that you miss valuable technical activity experience. The best DP professionals are detail-oriented and insist on full logic tables before coding. Because of the extensive use of software packages and utilities in the future, those who still can and will code will be more valued than those who claim to be above all that technical stuff. The so-called "bit twiddlers" are still the foot soldiers who win the wars.

Data processing technical professionals may eventually sacrifice their technical expertise for higher administrative positions. The risk in such an exchange is that they may not possess basic skills in managing others, and the return road to technical activities may be accompanied by a salary reduction and a psychological setback.

The technical software systems support area has a high risk for the DP professional, although higher initial earnings can be obtained there. The best jobs are often with computer manufacturers or software vendors or with large companies that have organized their own systems programming department. Seldom does the technical support specialist achieve the long-range recognition or salary of the management professional. Mastering technical support skills takes valuable career time. The internal software of any computer hardware has a limited life. Skill obsolescence can be a real danger as new computer technology develops. If the company changes vendors, specialists from the outside may obtain the key positions when new equipment arrives.

Company technical software programmers often trail the vendor software personnel simply because no information is disseminated. Clearly, there is less risk if the technical programmer is employed by a computer software vendor, because vendors must invest in training. The training budgets of user companies may be only the minimum necessary to maintain a system, and may not consider future needs. If you are a user company technical specialist for minor vendor equipment, your value to your company may be recognized, but the risk of skill obsolescence and restricted opportunities is clear.

The computer operations professional is charged with the day-to-day functional operation of computerized production. The computer center is a high exposure position. When production is on schedule, when reports are on time, when payroll checks are on time, the computer operations staff is frequently taken for granted. When technical complications or personnel problems prevent a smooth operation, however, many users and managers quickly rise to criticize without understanding the difficulties.

Frequently, a new system of computer programs must be set up by the operations staff to ensure the best utilization of existing computer hardware to fit within schedules and handle volume fluctuations. Computer operations staffs do not usually have an opportunity to achieve recognition commensurate with their value, even though millions of dollars are sometimes saved through more efficient operating methods.

The computer operations professional should maintain a complete record of his operational service improvements, performance statistics, and resulting savings to the company.

Computer Hardware

The number of vendor hardware models has increased significantly. Vendors have come and gone in the first twenty-five years of the computer age. Technical and marketing leadership is now concentrated in only a few vendors. The cost of computer power has dropped significantly. In order for you, the technical professional, to make the most of your career you should stay up to date on what is happening in computer hardware and on the success of certain vendors. It is to your advantage to have some experience and knowledge of the leading vendors' hardware. Table 3-4 is a representative list of computer hardware vendors and models. Some technical professionals cannot remember or perhaps have never learned the basic performance characteristics of computer hardware such as:

Mainframe performance factors
Input/output channel speeds
Data transfer rates
File access and delay times
File data capacities and transfer rates
Operating software memory requirements
Operating software overhead times

The mark of qualified technical professionals is knowledge of the economics of their computer hardware. Care should be taken not to spend too much of your career in a single hardware area because, like it, you can become obsolete. It takes about three years for you to become outdated if you have not stayed in the game. Computer hardware types and performance criteria are continually reported in *Auerbach* and *Data Professional literature.* * You should make use of the material produced by these professional computer reporting companies.

Clearly, any vendor hardware conferences and DP schools you can attend will give you wider general knowledge.

Table 3-4 Representative computer hardware vendors and models

Vendor	System Model
Amdahl Corp.	470/V6, 470/V8
Burroughs Corp.	B1700; B1800; B7800; B80
Control Data Corp.	Cyber 170; Omega 480; 3000 Series
Data General	Nova 3; Eclipse MY8000; System 10,20; Nova 1200
Data Point Corp.	1800; 5500; 6600
Digital Equipment Corp.	PDP11/45; VAX11/70; System 20; 500 VAX 11/780
Four Phase Systems	System IV/60
Hewlett-Packard	HP-250; HP2000; HP3000
Honeywell	H66/60; DPS8/44; 2000
IBM	370/XXX; System 1; 3; 32; 34; 38; 303X; 43XX
ICL (NASCO)	1900/L900 Series
ITEL	AS/7031, 8080/8085
Magnuson Computer Systems	M80/31
NAS/National Semiconductor	AS/3000, AS/5000, AS/7000, AS9000
NCR	400 Series; 7500 Series
Perkin Elmer	3220; 3240
Prime Computer	750
Sperry Rand (Univac)	V77-600; V77-800; U-90/30; U-1100/42; 9300, BC-7
Tandum Computers	Pathway
Texas Instruments	DS990/20/30
Wang Laboratories	VS-100; Series 2200
Xerox	530; 560

*Auerbach Computer Technology Reports, Pennsauken, NJ; Data Pro Research Corporation, Delran, NJ

Computer Operations Software

Operating systems software consists of common program routines to optimize computer hardware utilization and to eliminate repetitive coding. Systems software experience is essential to the technical DP professional. Credentials in system software include systems generations, internal software modifications, and macro coding to optimize and customize specific operational programs. Also included in the repertoire of the technical professional is work related to data base files. Experience in file design access routines and structures must be acquired early in your career. The true technical professional will not delay learning all phases of operational control and telecommunications software protocols. Representative computer operations software is displayed in Table 3-5. The best experience can be attained by working for a computer software vendor because a great deal of emphasis is placed on perfecting computer operational software.

The systems programmer will spend many hours learning the basic operating system of the installed hardware. Computer operations staff must also become fully conversant with utilizing computer-operating software because program running times can be materially affected.

Table 3-5 Representative computer operations software

Vendor	Operating Software
Burroughs	MCP; Gemcos
Data General	AOS
Datapoint	Databus; Data point
Digital Equipment Corp.	VAX/VMSII CTS-500; RSTS/E; ESX II; TOPS10/20; UNIX
Hewlett Packard	MPE
Honeywell	Gecos 8
IBM	OS; DOS; VS1; VS2; VM; JES; MFT; MVT; JCL; MVS
Microdata	Reality
NCR	VRX
Perkin Elmer	Reliance
Sperry Rand	OS-3
Texas Instruments	DX10

Computer Applications Software

Applications software is geared to creating business application programs and encompasses computer language, standard data base files, access routines, standard teleprocessing routines, and specialized application programs. Typically, specific business applications software is written expressly for a vendor's hardware and allows you to be more productive in preparing business application programs, sometimes merely by inserting parameters.

Computer applications specialists will find it beneficial to become proficient at using some of the computer software listed in Table 3-6. It is virtually impossible to be conversant with all computer languages; COBOL, assembler, or any communications and data base language will give you sufficient depth to be capable of learning any of the others. Be careful not to spread yourself so thin that you are the master of none. Equal care should be taken not to concentrate in one to the exclusion of all others. Either of these pitfalls can severely limit your range of job opportunities.

Business application software packages written by some of the software vendor leaders (Table 3-6) give you an excellent opportunity to learn about major business applications. There has never been an applications software package that did not require modification to some extent, but you may not want to make a career of it. You can acquire a great deal of knowledge quickly by contacting various software vendors and exploring their software on your own. Actively read publications such as *Computerworld* and *Datamation*. Here again *Auerback* and *Data Professional* publications can keep you abreast of new developments in application software. Don't neglect them. When you know how these packages work and can discuss them, you increase your market value considerably.

The purpose of this book is not to describe each of the computer hardware, operating, or application software types, only to indicate the scope of this expanding field. When you can associate the various software with respective vendors and describe what each does, you are on your way to becoming a professional. See how far you can complete Table 3-6. Over the next decade Table 3-6 will expand rapidly with a proliferation of companies and software specialities.

CONSULTING ACTIVITY

Many professional DP persons find it advantageous to sell their services as part-or full-time consultants. Once you have acquired a high skill level in a computer language, software packages, or business application areas, you may be surprised how much you can earn simply by asking for jobs in these areas. It is quite an easy matter simply to contact companies for information and make your proposal. Many applications-oriented individuals are a little unsure of themselves and never try.

First, it is difficult to perform a full-time job and find your next client at the same time. An easy way to find a client is to alert a good personnel agency to your availability and go on interviews they may arrange. You may

Table 3-6 Representative applications—software companies by software class
Programming Languages: COBOL, ASSEMBLER, FORTRAN IV-V, RPG II-III, APL, PL-1, ALGOL, PASCAL, BASIC, JOVIAL

Vendor	Data Bases	Data Communication	Data Retrieval	Production Control	Data Graphics	Resource Accounting	Programming Aids	Space Library Management	Business Applications
Applied Data Research		DATACOM/DB VOLLIE					ROSCOE		
Calcomp									
Cincom Systems, Inc.	TOTAL	ENVIRON/1							
Cullinane Corp.	IDMS	IDMS/DC	OL-QUERY CULPRIT			IDD	ESCAPE INTERACT		
IBM Corp.	IMS-DL-1	CICS, TCAM IMS/DC, CMS	DMS/CMS VM/IFS	POWER			TSO		CAD, DBOMP MRP CAM, COPICS MAPICS
Informatics			MARK IV						
Information Builders, Inc.			FOCUS						MISC
Intel Corp.	SYSTEM DDB 2000/80	DC						IDD	
Management & Computer Services							PROMACS		
Management Sciences/ America									FIN, PERSONNEL APPLS
Mathematica	RAMIS II	X	X				X		
National CCS, Inc.	NOMAD II								
NCR Comten		INTERFACE X.25							
On-Line Business Systems, Inc.							WYLBUR		
Panosophic Systems							EASYTRIEVE	PANVALET	
SAS Institute, Inc.					SAS Graph				
Software AG/North America	ADABAS	ADASCRIPT +					X		
University Computing Co.	UCC10			UCC2,7		RELIABILITY PLUS		UCC6	MISC

33

wish to join a consulting firm where you get exposure to many varied situations. If your marketing staff is good, there will be no lack of work, sometimes at higher pay than you would earn doing the same work with a company.

There are risks to your career, however. Your hours will be long and irregular which may affect your personal health, mental state, and social activities. If you are consulting full time, you may have to spend a considerable amount of time and money upgrading your skills. The lack of fringe benefits, paid vacations, company training, sick time, insurance, bonus, and pensions should be considered in your decision. There is a limit to the time and fees a person can charge. Companies can and do quickly terminate consulting contracts.

If you decide to try to expand your consulting activity, procuring additional good people will be a major problem. Managing new staff draws on different skills than doing all the work yourself.

Many consultants eventually try to return to work with companies as employees. Sometimes, depending on their consulting experience, good jobs can be procured. But many companies are reluctant to hire a consultant permanently because they believe it will only be a matter of time before the entrepreneur wants to be on his own again. Conservative managers may also be jealous of such industriousness.

If you are able to procure some long-term consulting contracts with past employers or good companies, you may do well, but you had better be a good salesman. If you simply work for a consulting firm, they will not need you after the contract runs out. Unless you can get new business for them you may find yourself looking for a permanent employer. It might be better to establish a promotional career with a company.

Because of the close association between business data processing and accounting activity, CPA firms have been entering the DP field through separate divisions called management services. These firms perform activities and sell services ranging from DP auditing to DP requirements planning to systems design to full-scale DP project implementations. Some CPA firms even market their own software packages and sell them to their client firms. Sometimes it is difficult to see how so-called independent auditors can get away with selling systems to audit their own work and then get paid to certify it. Since many of these firms are actively placing their own staff in client companies, their own people can carry out the installation of their previous employer's software. It makes you wonder, doesn't it? Frequently, these firms select younger, inexperienced, but bright college graduates to learn on client companies' time at high fees. If you can obtain a job like this, it is a very valuable learning experience. People orientation is a key to a successful consulting career. Look forward to lots of travel.

Remember Wesler's law of consulting: nothing is impossible for the person who doesn't have to do it.

1 The DP consultant is hired—an expert in computers.
2 The computer data center is built—but does not work.
3 To get it to work, a budget is needed.
4 To get the budget, the computer must become productive.
5 The DP consultant moves on.

MARKETING ACTIVITY

Another specialized DP experience that can draw on DP knowledge is marketing hardware and software. Clearly, success in this specialty hinges on whether the product development group of the vendor has hit the target market at the right time. Hardware and software marketing gives a wide range of experience and provides opportunity for high pay—with corresponding high risk. Marketing skills are frequently diametrically opposed to technical skills. Since selling is more emotional and psychological, the best technicians are frequently the poorest salesmen, and vice versa.

If your company handles a wide range of hardware, software, and services, you can learn a wide range of skills. It takes a special DP professional to achieve a good career in marketing. Many successful and not-so-successful computer marketing types have moved directly to the top of the pyramid, without passing go, because they were in the right place at the right time and were good communicators. Some succeed and some fail because they had not developed the basics of management or the technical depth required. There continues to be high demand for successful DP marketing people. If pressure quotas are your thing, do it. You will trade security for opportunity.

SCIENTIFIC PROGRAMMING

The scientific programmers (SP) are generally technical specialists in a field such as engineering, chemistry, psychology, medicine, physics, operations research, or statistics. They are not normally concerned with data flow, manual procedures, or file designs. Scientific programmers normally use their talent in specialized fields to computerize solutions to ongoing problems, or to one-shot problems that have specific solutions or ranges.

The SP normally does not become a business data processor. This field is more narrow and deep, akin to that of the technical support DP professional. Its primary computer languages include FORTRAN, PL-1, APL, and ALGOL.

PERSONAL CAPABILITY

Your personal attributes, education, skills, and preferences will determine your selection of a career area in data processing. The job class or level, business applications, systems activities, technical activities, hardware and software knowledge are the components of DP experience. Each experience will allow you to build toward the top of the pyramid, depending on your orientation, preference, and skill.

It is clear that certain DP job classifications demand more people orientation than creative talents. Other DP job classifications demand more mechanical aptitude than social skills. You may want to consider the job areas displayed in Table 3-7 when you are making fundamental choices regarding a DP career from the point of view of your personal reward preference and capabilities.

The DP pyramid head may have begun his career as a programmer, but he then had to develop other orientations to achieve more responsibility and earnings.

Table 3-7 Data processing orientation preference

Orientation	Job	Operations	Programming	Software	Systems	Management
Data	(What?)		X		X	X
People	(Who?)	X			X	X
Ideas	(Why?)			X	X	X
Mechanics	(How?)	X	X	X	X	X

SUMMARY

This chapter aims to help you think of the many alternatives offered by a DP career. Many professionals are so buried in their day-to-day activities that they forget where they are going. Perhaps it's so much fun that they do not particularly care. After all, it's only their life, their family, and their future.

By understanding the full range of DP activities you can make better plans and choices for your future. You must analyze yourself and determine those areas in which you excel. In some cases you will not know until you try. Certainly, some job levels and experience areas will give you more earnings than others, only if you can compete. But you should never select a job if you do not have the basic aptitudes to do well in it. Salary should never be the sole guide in your choice of a career in EDP.

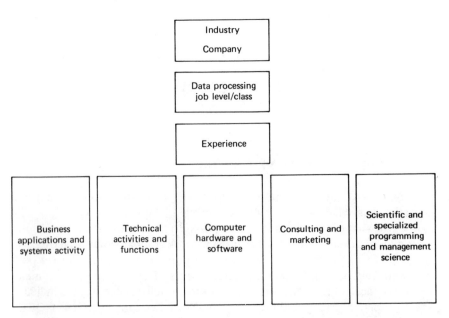

Salary surveys in DP are available from many sources, categorized frequently by DP job name and section of the country. These surveys are conducted by DP personnel placement agencies, market research firms, publishers, and government agencies.

While surveys provide useful guidelines, they can never apply to you directly. What you are worth is what an employer is willing to pay you at a particular point in time. You may get more than the going rate simply because you are available and no one else is at that time but the opposite is also true. A company may simply like you better than your competition. You may have just the right mix of experience they need at that moment.

Now you are in a position to decide what experience you want to obtain. Getting it is the next problem. But before you start planning, you should know something about what companies do with regard to DP personnel and their acquisition and treatment. Don't ever think that what you want will be awarded by any company without a price.

Four

Learn Company Tactics and
Use Them to Your Advantage

WHAT COMPANIES WANT AND DO

Companies vary in their requirements for DP professionals. Often they are not sure themselves what qualities are needed. Frequently a company will not know what human qualities are required to accomplish the DP mission, or it may not even know what the mission is. A company may advertise for a DP professional with one kind of background and eventually hire a person who only partially meets the requirements. The personnel department résumé, collectors frequently don't know how to tell a superior DP candidate from a superior résumé, and the best résumé often gets the interview. NOTE: An ex-pro quarterback might get called before a professional programmer because someone heard that Dallas uses a computer to test football plays. Ridiculous? Maybe. Nevertheless the principle is valid. Examine some of the following variables in the employee selection process. The following are not necessarily indictments of companies, but simply show what happens when some organizations try to manage DP activity with inadequate employee selection criteria.

Testing

Many companies place emphasis on DP aptitude tests. Seldom do these tests, designed to indicate EDP aptitude, really reveal who can perform various DP jobs best in the real world. Most tests show those who can pass tests.

Competency of DP personnel selected for jobs is defined frequently and *erroneously* in terms of job aspects, job descriptions, competence in a parallel type of job over a long period of time on similar computer hardware and software.

Only infrequently do companies select or promote DP personnel on the basis of those "characteristics and traits of people" that contribute to

38

accomplishing the job best. Selection cirteria such as aggressiveness, attractiveness, personal friends, perceived ambitions, willingness to try unrealistic jobs hardly seem appropriate.

Realistic competency evaluation for DP personnel seems to be a long way off. There is little correlation among computer science school aptitude scores, professional DP performance, and success. The hiring and training of more competent DP personnel sometimes may not be possible because in most companies the organizational structure does not permit encouragement of and reward for DP competency characteristics. The mediocre prevail.

Education

Most companies prefer job candidates to have a college degree because it is believed that a degreed person will absorb company training better and will be a more valuable and promotable long-term employee. Degrees in computer science and quantitative methods applied to business problems are the first choice. Advanced DP degrees do not necessarily carry more weight with a company. Technical and business degrees with computer programming courses are almost equally in demand. After three to five years in data processing, a degree becomes less important if the DP professional has remained in the technical activity. Computer vendor schools and hardware and software knowledge then predominate. A programmer with a degree in a specialized area, such as finance, may not make the most of his specialty if he simply takes on any DP job assignments that come along.

Strangely enough, the school grade-point average does not appear to make a significant difference in starting salaries. In fact, computer programming trainees with only an associate (two-year) certificate often start with salaries equivalent to those possessing a four-year degree.

As the DP professional approaches the manager level, the power of the degree surfaces. Companies often select managers only from among degreed DP personnel. Seldom does a person without a degree climb to the top of a major DP pyramid, even if the degree is in basket weaving.

Companies are always impressed by people who continue their DP career education in evening school. A position with a company that does not require a degree is usually regarded as a dead-end job.

The Institute of Certification of Computer Professionals (ICCP) offers a certificate in data processing (CDP) and a certificate in computer programming (CCP). The importance of these certificates is increasing, although in the eyes of most companies they are far from equalling certificates of the accounting profession, such as that for a certified public accountant (CPA), or for a certified managerial accountant (CMA). Most professions do depend for their substance on criteria such as public practice and responsibility, a code of ethics, a definable body of knowledge, and standards, and EDP seems to qualify in this respect as a profession. Some companies sponsor examination review courses for candidates for CDP and CCP. Many schools that offer degrees in computer science train their graduates well enough so they can pass these examinations without special reviews. In summary, certificates are valued by some companies more than by others, but it may be that the more letters you can accumulate on your résumé the better off you are. It is this author's belief that until these certificates become really tough to get, they will be considered worthless by companies. Standards probably won't be raised until a legal license to practice is required, perhaps based on industry standards, problems, and practices. Since the only real standard developed in the computer industry to date has been the keypunch card symbol, it may be a long time before the DP industry establishes standards of performance—and their corresponding wage scale.

Personal Attributes and Images

Many companies like Boy Scout types. Personal attributes such as speech, dress, appearance, cordiality, conversational seriousness, humaneness, self-restraint, and salesmanship may get you a good position even if you are short in some technical qualifications. Some companies may even create a position for you, if you are their type of person. You may simply be someone with whom they would like to go fishing. Consulting firms demand a professional image, because you represent the firm in the client's office. Everything about you must evoke professionalism. Interpersonal skills may override many technical deficiences, but technical skills will never override personal deficiencies.

Bosses tend to hire and keep people like themselves. An opposite would probably be a better choice—as a counterbalance—but we are all human, after all. If the boss plays golf and your score is high, if you play chess and he is a grandmaster, if you play football and he coaches, if you both went to the University of Illinois, you have an edge over other candidates. He will train you—no problem. Be sure your image closely parallels that of your boss.

DISCRIMINATION FACTORS

Clearly, discriminatory hiring and promotional practices often exist, even in data processing. Among these are:

Age	If you are over forty and not at the managerial level, it's too late to worry about it.
Sex	If you are female, you can always find functional jobs, but your chances of becoming a manager of men are not equal. You are acceptable as a *supervisor* of women.
Name	If you have a name indicating an ethnic background, change it.
Marital status	If you are married you are okay. If you are single and past thirty, you are odd or a swinger. Divorce is acceptable but not at the managerial level, unless you have been there for five years.
Appearance	If you are ugly, you had better be good. If you are handsome you are in until you are forty. If you are sloppy, you have had it even if they say they want a shirtsleeves type. If you are overweight, you will get less money and lose opportunities. If your haircut is not right for your age, fix it. Always dress for success, even on the third shift.
Job tenure	If you have changed jobs every year, you are more suspect than those who have three-year terms with some in-house promotions. You have a problem.
Language	If your words are clear and crisp you are better than the "grunt," "huh" types. If you can communicate and sell yourself, you know it and they know it. "You know what I mean" types cannot communicate. Four-letter words label you quickly.
Psychological factors	People who can smile and go easy are better than uptight and aloof types. If you are dead serious about your work you are ahead of the cynics and jokers. If you know who quarterbacks the San Diego Chargers, you are okay. Make your sexual advances off the premises.
Scores	If you score high on company tests or have received honors, awards, and leadership plaques, you are wanted.

Personal attributes	Intelligence	Creativity	Objectives
	Honesty	Ambition	Goals
	Motivation	Ability to listen	Attention span
	Likability	Ability to talk	Memory
	Competence	High golf scores	Independence

Personal attributes make the difference. Know yourself.

Salary Levels

Companies believe your current earnings are a measure of your growth and present worth. Systematic progress is all-important. Questions will be asked if you are working either below or above a normal market value for your age or experience at given job levels and classes.

Many companies hire on an unrealistic DP budget. The personnel department may have acquired a DP salary survey and established a false set of salary ranges for DP job classes and levels. Instead of paying for an exceptional person with a productive capacity of three, two persons, each with a capability of one, are hired. After all, head-counts build empires. Some think paying the going rate attracts and keeps good professionals. Wrong. It keeps the mediocre.

Progressive companies create positions for individuals they find, instead of forcing exceptional data processors into preestablished job descriptions and salary ranges. The best companies have open-ended DP salary ranges. Companies frequently believe that budgets and salary ranges control DP salaries. Wrong. The market controls salaries and companies match the group rate or get out. A progressive company will never pass up an exceptional individual for an extra thousand dollars. Companies spend that much on stationery in the personnel department, advertisements, and applicant travel expenses.

Generally, companies want to acquire the best possible candidate, but at the lowest possible cost. It is important not to earn too much above the going rate in your job level or class, or you will risk being replaced by someone from the outside who will work at a lower rate. Try not to accept a position where your salary is at the top of the range, because then only a promotion can get you a good pay increase within the company.

Management Experience

Companies often attempt to evaluate a candidate's potential by examining the level of management experience he has obtained over a period of years. They value an orderly progression through increasing amounts of responsibility and are wary of those who have not served their time in positions in higher management. While time alone is not a measure of managerial competence, the DP director who has never written a COBOL program, operated a computer, or managed a project development team is highly suspect, unless he is the son of the vice president. Many DP professionals are competent in dealing with computers but lack the ability to deal with people.

Functional Skills

Many companies value functional skills highly. The quantity and quality of functional data processing work you can produce is easily measured. For example:

An 18,000 per hour keystroke rate with zero errors

Five hundred lines of debugged code produced per day

Ninety-five percent CPU utilization by the operations department

Professional DP functionaries know their production rate, because it is easily converted into a dollar rate of pay. In functional jobs, attendance, reliability, comprehension, and exactness mean a great deal. Proximity to the work site and personal transportation mean you can help more readily in times of peak loads or emergency. Willingness to work overtime or second shift makes you more valuable.

Where functional skills are emphasized, such attributes as creativity, knowledge, education, judgment, and social skills are not of prime importance. In functional DP jobs, the company is hiring a human machine, not a person. The length of time spent in a job grade can have some effect on the pay rate, regardless of how productive you are, but only up to a point.

Hardware and Software Experience

Many company managers are hung up on the specific hardware/software of the company, regardless of the job level or the actual technical depth required for a particular position. Hardware and software background will often be specified in terms of a vendor and experience in terms of years. For many jobs at lower levels, specialized equipment and software experience can get you an immediate interview and job, since many companies do not care to train anyone. Frequently it matters little how much experience a DP professional has in alternate vendor equipment or software, experience that could easily be a basis for learning the company's computer machinery. Clearly, these companies are hiring a functionary for immediate skills rather than investing in a long-term qualified person. This policy may get you an initial salary increase, but you may be discarded when the need for your skill subsides or the company changes equipment. You may be phased into maintaining the old programs, while new personnel are brought in to accelerate new computer program development.

Business Applications

Experience in common business applications is clearly expected by hiring companies. Systems development activities in business applications support evidence of experience, (see Table 3-2). Companies will hire a DP professional to utilize his special application experience to enhance their own corresponding business applications. If your background is ahead of their development, you have definite leverage to get a good offer. Be sure you know your strengths in relation to their systems.

Self Presentation

Your ability to display your total self in the above-mentioned areas will help the company to determine whether you really have what they want. If you are successful in clearly presenting your experience, you may get an offer above your expectations. If a company does not like you or your presentation, your experience buys you less, regardless of how good it is. Company practices are never perfect. Some companies are better organized in their management of data processing activities than others. What companies want is rarely what they get. Love is ideal, but marriage is real. Frequently, companies hire and promote those they like rather than those who are best qualified.

Promotions, Pay and Training

In some companies, DP promotion from within is a lip-service myth. When management perceives that a change is needed because of a lack of progress or for political reasons, one group of adversaries is usually replaced. If you are on the team of a losing manager, you had better plan your future and pick a new boss, or get a transfer. Its called reorganization.

Bosses become very protective of good producers and they frequently succeed in clamping on the "golden handcuffs." In this situation you are earning too much to be considered for any other experience-building positions in the company. Some DP professionals do not realize this until it is too late. Then they must take a pay reduction to gain breadth of experience so they can proceed upward again. Some may instead trade their career to maintain their short-term standard of living. Two to three years is the limit you can wait for a promotion.

Few companies have true career paths planned for DP professionals, probably because the planners know little about EDP and the DP management is too busy to establish the structure required to attract, acquire, and keep a top-quality DP staff. Frequently, DP personnel budgets are set as a percentage of sales and no thought is given to the critical supply of and demand for DP personnel in the market or the upward movement of DP salaries. Data processing salaries are often pegged to the other salary levels in the company. If accountants are content with 4 percent raises this year, so should the DP staff. Wrong! The hidden costs of turnover, advertising, new hiring, training, and reruns are swept quietly under the rug by many company personnel departments because they have not learned how to display these costs to company management effectively. Only when the computer stops do they rush into action. Conversely, many large, high-quality companies have excellent DP programs and consequently have attracted and kept many of the best DP professionals in the United States. They know what they are doing. This activity of large companies has of course made it doubly difficult for smaller companies to compete for the less-competent remainder, but it has kept salaries moving up for everyone. These quality companies have good training programs and varied assignments and they frequently pay full tuition for those who are able to pursue evening courses. In some cases, good DP personnel are paid to pursue additional training on a released-time basis at full pay.

Last but not least, good companies have formal pay reviews, including standards of promotion and pay increases. Companies with formal reviews show clearly their concern for planning and evaluation of your worth. You should question companies that give you pay raises only at their discretion and have no planned written reviews. Ask to look at the formal review forms. Are they superficial or do they address the rating of your performance based on agreed-upon objectives, goals, and formal standards of accomplishment in DP work. Ask what you have to do this year to receive a substantial pay increase or a promotion to the next job level. If the company can't tell you or tells you just to keep your politics clean, you are with a loser.

Terminations

Some companies plan turnover by allowing you to reach your salary range limit, after which no subsequent higher level exists. Then they simply explain that they are cutting back, and you are terminated. Some DP professionals fail to see that they have been fired. They continue on for years with minimal raises and meaningless assignments and responsibilities. The company has already slotted them for departure, preferably before any retirement benefits have to be paid. Age soon takes its toll, and alternate in-house jobs become impossible to find.

Assignments and Practices

Many DP personnel careers become trapped by the needs of the company. Maintenance of a current system is an example. While others build the new system, you are stuck maintaining the old system until you are no longer needed. If you spend a year putting out fires or making minor enhancements without a definite date set for your new assignment, you should take a close look at your market value. Maintenance experience buys you less than new-program-development experience.

Some companies structure data-input and computer operations as split and rotating shifts. Only part-time personnel may be used, so that benefits need not be provided. This reduces the ability of functional operators to procure a second job or even search for one. Programmers are sometimes called programmer analysts so that they legally won't have to be paid overtime and can work on Saturdays without pay—all for the big carrot that never materializes. Companies will tend to keep you slotted in a position that benefits company operations. Fourteen-hour days without overtime pay is sometimes expected of you. A few lawsuits against this practice have been successful. Forget about those companies as career opportunities.

Sometimes only the departure of several key people will lead to a revision of work assignment policies and salary schedules. Generally, personnel departments will not assume responsibility for not having watched DP assignments, hours, or salaries closely enough. Also, some personnel departments simply do not have the power to address DP management practices. In order to protect the company, exit interviews will always reflect reasons for termination other than the actual ones. A typical one is "You know how computer types are"—whatever that means! It usually means that DP people have a better knowledge than personnel departments of exploitative job policies. Supply and demand take their toll.

Some company managers have unwritten agreements that they will not hire computer specialists from each other. This means that competition ceases to exist and practices can continue as usual. Sometimes such a company will inform another company if it receives a résumé from one of its competitor's employees. Some companies pay up to 10 percent over the going rate to ensure the captivity of good professionals. They will cut your pay later. In order to protect an account, computer vendors will seldom hire from one of their good customers. They will hire from each other. In fact, they will inform on you if they know you are looking. They may even think they are doing you a favor by alerting your management.

Projects

Participation in new systems projects can be the most effective way up the pyramid. Systems projects often follow patterns that can be described as phases:

Phase 1   Wild enthusiasm in hiring (experts and consultants)

Phase 2   Disillusionment with perceived schedules
Phase 3   Total confusion under pressure (management)
Phase 4   The search for the guilty (who is to blame)
Phase 5   The punishment of the innocent (those that are left)
Phase 6   The promotion of the nonparticipants (the master politicians)
Phase 7   Installed, but not with promised results (the functionaries)

While the above phases may get a knowledgeable chuckle from those who have been through some fiascos in systems development, it is clear that millions of dollars have been spent by some companies only to have the new president ask "Why did we ever do that?" The answers range from "It seemed like a good idea at the time" to "We simply don't know" to "The DP professional was a good salesman."

Good projects follow developmental phases described in many texts as follows:

Current system definition
New requirements planning
New system design
Computer hardware and software selection
Economics evaluation and redesign
Conversion planning
Manual and computer program specifications
Computer programming/testing
System user training
System testing and conversion
System implementation
System evaluation

Several of these phases are divided into subphases.

The point to be made is that major projects can fail if detail planning is not done extremely well and if the project does not have the full support of management and the functional users. You must know the status of the project along the way. If any of the phases are cut short or are not properly executed, your project team may be. Improperly planned and scheduled projects can get so pressured that your teammates leave, and their burden is placed on you. The dilemma arises because so much knowledge is accumulated along the way; if key project members leave, it is virtually impossible to acquire new staff and maintain the project schedule originally established.

Watch out for managements which are not sympathetic to this situation. If the project is messed up, your career will suffer. If it is successful, you will progress. There is nothing so pathetic in an interview as having to explain why two years of your career were spent in a system failure, even if you were only a small part of it. Even your best references will have to admit that things just didn't go well. You had better know if your company and its DP management have ever planned or been through a major project before. If a project is disintegrating before your very eyes, you had better have sense enough to get out while you are still on your feet. Some dumb managements apply whips, asking for twenty-five-hour days and all weekends to prove that they can make things happen. Your blood, their guts. Outside of shear boredom, the turmoil of the pressure caused by poor planning is probably the most important cause of DP turnover. As Kipling said, "More good men are killed by overwork than the importance of the world justifies."

Companies think new systems will work well; in reality, they generally work poorly or not at all. New computer systems do not change the way things are done in most companies but only speed things up. New systems tend to grow up primarily to kill new problems that the system itself has generated. They seldom meet the new requirements originally perceived. More paper, more volume, and more higher-priced technical help spur on new technology so that the system cycle can be repeated. If a system is working, leave it alone. The DP plan often fails to consider that the single most important factor in success is the procurement of the best DP personnel. First and foremost, a capable DP person to lead the effort must be found. He must be able to:

1   Win the respect and confidence of top management
2   Attract competent people
3   Utilize his staff effectively

Many companies spend a fortune on computer hardware and software, then hire dummies to make it all work.

ELECTRONIC DATA PROCESSING RECRUITING

Many companies do not start their EDP recruiting until someone has departed and left a workload gap for the remaining professionals to fill by unpaid overtime. If the manpower does not exist, the health of the staff is sacrificed for the company, obviously, lower-quality work generates more maintenance and reruns. If that is your company situation you are with a loser.

Newspaper ads are then placed describing the company and the available job. Applicants often miss these ads or are not able to move at the time of a company's needs. Good companies can sometimes rely on personal referrals or bonuses to bring in qualified EDP professionals. This can be a very effective means for hiring competent people. Some company personnel departments do an excellent job of attracting qualified applicants and of presenting both their company and the job. Other personnel departments fail even to respond to applicant inquiries. Quality companies eventually answer all inquiries.

Some companies use blind ads. They hope to get a flood of high-quality DP people. Actually, blind ads get only a low-quality and low-quantity response. Top people do not answer blind ads; there are many résumé collectors, and it may be their own company's ad. In fact, it may result in their résumé being sent back to their boss from a consultant or auditor of their own company. Of course, if you are unemployed, anything goes. But when you go blind, you generally lose.

Good DP professionals are never unemployed but rather, are "available" to look at exceptional opportunities—not, however, through blind ads. Frequent open ads by the same company indicate it has trouble getting and keeping good people. Even in open ads, the chances are slim of acquiring a person with all the right qualifications. Usually, after a week or two ad qualifications are reduced, and sometimes the next warm body in the door gets the job. Figures 4-1 to 4-9 show some types of DP ads. Have

---

THE AD

BEGINNERS/TRAINEES

Hurry, complete training program starting soon
B.S. comp science, math, acctg
Call Sam (212) 888-5000   Fee paid
Krapp Agency 656 Main St.   Troy N.J.

OBSERVATIONS

1 Seldom can agencies collect fees for beginners.
2 They may want to meet so you can tell them where you have been and what's going on.
3 They want your résumé so they can handle your placement in a year, after you are experienced.
4 There is nothing like a few wild goose chases.
5 It is better to call large companies direct for training programs.
6 Does a job really exist?

Figure 4-1 Job advertisement analysis.

you ever noticed that most companies say only what they want, not what they will give you? Most give very little attention to EDP career planning.

When résumés are received by companies, they are frequently reviewed first by the personnel department. Preliminary judgments based on job descriptions, required experience, and DP jargon are made to exclude those not meeting the specifications. If some résumés appear stronger, chances are that the others will be filed away or discarded. If there is heavy response to an ad, you may get only a cursory examination—hence the importance of a good, clear résumé. Once your résumé has been filed, the chances are slim that you will be called in because it is very costly to research hundreds of old résumés.

Even if the perfect job, for which you would qualify, should open up a month later, it is unlikely that you will be remembered. The company may

---

THE AD

PROGRAMMER/SYSTEM ANALYST

Where Are You?

I have the following positions:

OS/DOS COBOL Programmers	$ 15–25K
BAL Progs/SR	$ 25–35K
RSX 11, UAX RSTS/E Progs	$ 20–35K
DP Manager	$ 28–35K
Mark 4 Programmers	$ 20–30K
CICS Specialists	$ 25–35K

Call Al Expert 889-5222

Fast Place Agency

568 MPC/88th St.   Fees Paid

OBSERVATIONS

1 The law says that any jobs advertised by an agency must really be open.
2 The jobs may be in different states.
3 This is truly a laundry list. The agency must have a low overhead.
4 The job salary ranges are too wide to ring true for real jobs.
5 The companies must be shotgunning: They will take anyone in a wide range.
6 Some of the companies want you for "right now" skills.
7 What do you get? They don't tell you that. Only money?

Figure 4-2   Job advertisement analysis.

assume that you have taken another job after you sent in your résumé, and DP management is simply too busy to do follow-up. For this reason, if you really want to look into a job or company, follow up your résumé with a phone call to the DP manager himself.

Outstanding résumés get passed upward. The importance of the neat résumé is obvious. If appropriate résumés are not received in response to the company ad, the company may place it again or simply decide to use a DP agency. Of course, all this resumania can take from two weeks to two months to slog through the company administration. The personnel department recruits for the whole company.

If you are in a hurry, forget it. The major DP agents will have three of your competitors set up for interviews two days after the ad runs, frequently interviews with the decision maker. You may ask how your friend got an interview when you sent your résumé in two weeks before. He was properly exposed and sold to the right person. You were not. Perhaps someone was out of town, in meetings, or on vacation or overlooked some factor on

---

THE AD

DATA PROCESSING SUPERVISOR

Washington, D.C., headquarters of a Fortune 200 company has immediate opening for data processing supervisor to manage business computer installation. Should have 4–6 years DP experience in systems and programming, project management application system experience in financial and accounting systems a must. Position requires a person having good communication skills, ability to interface with management, and able to operate with a minimum of supervison. Salary commensurate with experience. Send résumé and salary history to:

Box 6969 Post

OBSERVATIONS

1   Jobs names and positions are not clarified.
2   Since when does a supervisor operate with a minimum of supervision unless it's an operating job?
3   If it's operations, then why 4–6 years experience? Do you want more of the same for another 4 years?
4   If it's operations, why is systems development background required?
5   The salary looks like the minimum they can get you for.
6   What's the promotional path?
7   Why won't they identify themselves? Most large companies do.
8   This might be a blind résumé collector.

Figure 4-3   Job advertisement analysis.

your résumé. If all they have is a piece of paper, it had better be a good one. Sometimes, company ads work in EDP recruiting.

Using Agencies

Sooner or later the knowledgeable manager realizes that the search for DP professionals can be enhanced by the use of a good DP employment agency. Many long-term relationships exist between companies and agencies. Good agencies continually advertise and have long-standing relationships with quality applicants, who register but who want to be contacted only for exceptional opportunities. Companies know that good agencies can aggressively sell or blackball them and can pinpoint, recruit, and sell good people on the company. A reputable company will not raid DP personnel of another company.

Many DP professionals will not apply to a company because it is unfamiliar to them, or because they could not qualify for the job as described

---

THE AD

SOFTWARE MANAGER

Real-Time Computer Control Systems

Supervise a team of computer specialists involved in the design and development of computerized traffic control systems. Applicants must have 4–6 years direct involvement in systems engineering and programming of real-time applications on general-purpose minicomputers. Intimate knowledge of real-time operating systems and FORTRAN and assembly programming languages. Knowledge of traffic control hardware operations desirable. Occasional travel. Salary negotiable, based on qualifications.

Call or send résumé: (607) 496-4320

Signal Systems   Sackhack, N.J. 07601

Equal Opportunity Employer M/F

OBSERVATIONS

1 The company identifies itself and the job, and the phone number indicates they are moving fast.
2 The company knows what it wants.
3 If you have the background, you could get a good salary.
4 It's worth a collect call.
5 Since there is no agency fee, you could get a good offer.
6 The job is probably located in New Jersey, but the remote plants probably exist, requiring travel.

Figure 4-4   Job advertisement analysis.

in terms of the ideal applicant, or because the job is given an obscure title. For many reasons, a greater number of DP professionals utilize personnel agents than do other professionals. One important reason is that most DP jobs are so time-consuming that there simply is no time to search effectively on your own for the next career position. It is easier to place your order with a good agent (insist on what you want your next career step to be) and wait till the right job opens up. Since good jobs are hard to find even in data processing, it could take six months to a year to find it. Personnel departments are frequently hostile toward DP agents. They feel that their jobs are being impinged upon, even though they often do not understand DP psychology or the technical job. Personnel departments that utilize all avenues of DP recruiting are probably the most effective.

Obviously, some companies dislike paying fees to an agency, but they realize that the right person in the job means an immediate saving, much more than the relatively small fee. Contrary to popular belief, a company does not have to pay an applicant less because an agency fee was paid. One-time costs can never be compared to ongoing costs, even in introductory accounting. Agency fees are tax-deductible expenses. The agency fees are very low compared to most personnel department advertising and recruiting budgets.

THE AD

WINTER IN FLORIDA

Co.-paid relocation
Sr P.A.'s & project leader types
IBM COBOL OS a must—on-line a plus
Salary $25–36K
Call/come in Monday
Sam Trap/Al Clincher
891-3780
Scenario Agency

OBSERVATIONS

1 They have a company in Florida for which they are recruiting for several levels of jobs.
2 On-line experience could be obtained.
3 The company is probably running its own ads too, since many positions need to be filled.
4 If you can go direct, their offer might be better.
5 The job could be in Miami or Pensacola.

Figure 4-5   Job advertisement analysis.

Some companies do ask an applicant to pay or share the agency fee. Avoid these companies and situations from the beginning. Top DP agencies deal only with companies that pay the entire fee.

When a top agency gets an order for a specific job class or level, it will immediately check out its registrants. Experienced agents can immediately call their registered applicants for an updated résumé and review the general characteristics of the job opportunity without identifying the company. They will always obtain the applicants permission to send a résumé or to discuss his background with a client company. Some agencies are ruthless, simply boiler-plating your résumé and send it to every company in town. *It will soon get back to your company.* A good agency will present a complete background on you to a company the same day the order is placed, if you are available. Also, companies know that the large national EDP agencies can often tell them about qualified applicants in other cities. National coverage gives them a larger choice of applicants, even though there may be interview travel costs and relocation expenses. Since these costs are in most cases, charged to the personnel department budget, DP management likes to have the larger choice of candidates. Large agency offices talk to their nearby peers daily and know who is available for both close and distant moves. There is a higher probability that applicants who move shorter distances will remain longer with their new company, and so agencies generally prefer to present candidates from nearby cities.

THE AD

CICS CONSULTANTS

Startreck, A national software consultant with a staff of 600 and 24 branches, is recruiting CICS systems designers, systems programmers, and programmer analysts for client accounts in Chicago, Cleveland, Detroit, Minneapolis, and Pittsburgh.

If you want to join a specialist team developing and installing new systems and client training and you have at least 2 + years experience in CICS, BAL, or COBOL contact Joe Techman.

OBSERVATIONS

1 Narrow and deep specialization.
2 Trade breadth of experience for money.
3 What replaces CICS?
4 Probably lots of travel.
5 Not necessarily a move up the pyramid.

Figure 4-6   Job advertisement analysis.

It is advantageous to be registered with a quality EDP placement agency on a "true promotional opportunity" basis. You will constantly be apprised of the market and what is happening in data processing throughout the country.

Executive Recruiting

Some companies use the service of executive search organizations. Search firms are generally paid higher than normal fees and out-of-pocket expenses to go after the right individuals, wherever they may be. The firms are generally paid whether or not the candidate is hired. They are used when:

High-level positions are to be filled
The candidate has a rare combination of attributes
Personal chemistry is important

THE AD

SUPERVISOR, PROGRAMMING SYSTEMS

DOS/VS installation looking for qualified individual experienced in PL/1 data base/data communications CICS/VS and manufacturing business systems. If you have a BS degree, 5-6 years of data processing experience, and supervisory experience in business system programming and computer systems management, this opportunity is for you. We are a highly respected capital goods manufacturer which will provide a competitive wage and attractive fringe benefits to the right candidate. Please send a confidential résumé, including salary history to:

Box NNA 329, Tribune

OBSERVATIONS

1   A smaller shop growing up (DOS) conversion to (OS)?
2   PL/1, CICS/VS? State of Art OS?
3   A lateral if you meet requirements of supervision.
4   Respected vs. Fast growing?
5   Competitive vs. excellent wage?
6   Relies on fringes.
7   Why not identified? Turnover high? Promote from within?
8   Probably just another job.
9   What do you learn? Where do you go next?

Figure 4-7   Job advertisement analysis.

A clean sweep of present personnel is coming
An urgent need exists
The highest confidentiality is required
Specific companies are to be raided

If you are contacted by a search firm, they will generally ask whether you know of anyone fitting certain requirements. Obviously, this will be flattering to you because it indicates that someone has recommended you as a person "in the know." It may be you they are after, or simply references. The chances are that they have a good job opening, and it is always to your advantage to cooperate discreetly. Always call them back, never spill your knowledge on the first call. You must determine that the call is from a legitimate search firm. If you do know of some top people, they should compensate you for your time and effort. Why shouldn't you negotiate part of the big fee? Tell them you will make the contact—you may be able to use their help in the future.

THE AD

DATA PROCESSING $35,000

"Manager Systems and Programming." The highly paid professional we hire will have a strong background in financial system with a bachelor's/master's degree in computer science or accounting. Three years' experience in large IBM environment is essential, as is knowledge of COBOL and assembler. The position we offer requires a performance-oriented executive with superior communication skills ready to accept challenge and responsibility. A major corporation in Tim Buck Tu, we offer a state-of-the-art environment plus an outstanding package of benefits plus compensation. Candidates interested in an exciting future with a company known for innovation and development should submit confidential résumé and salary history to:

Box 999, *Chronicle*
(Equal Opportunity Employer)

OBSERVATIONS

1 Well-written ad could mean good company.
2 They know what they want and have taken the time to describe it.
3 Worth an answer, but not with your résumé. Describe your background only and give your phone number without salary attached.
4 It could be a search firm.
5 Probably replacing the present manager.

Figure 4-8 Job advertisement analysis.

THE AD

SENIOR VICE PRESIDENT
Information Resource Management

We're the Security Bank of Mid-America and our ambition counts on yours. We're now the most heavily funded bank in the world. There is a newly created spot for a Senior V.P. for our Chicago-based data center.

Ideal candidate will have 15 years of data processing experience with at least 10 years in DP management and 5 years managing the systems development and data center function. Your background should include in-depth knowledge of systems design, data base/data communication systems, state-of-the-art technology, networking, hardware and software evaluations, and data center operations. Most essential is large-scale IBM hardware and software environment and supervision (within the last five years) of a minimum of 150–200 people. A BS in business, mathematics, or engineering is required, but an MBA is preferred.

We offer an attractive and highly competitive salary along with comprehensive benefits.

John Xwire   918 Michigan Avenue   Chicago Illinois

OBSERVATIONS

1 The top of the pyramid.
2 Don't try for it without bank experience and an MBA.
3 There are not too many of these jobs advertised openly. Most of these positions are filled through search firms and references within the industry.

Figure 4-9   Job advertisement analysis.

SUMMARY

This chapter aims to help you understand some company DP job practices and actions. You can evaluate and plan your DP future more effectively if you are aware of your own company's tactics. It is clearly advantageous for you to navigate successfully up the pyramid within your own company. In your early years as a professional, you can easily leave one company for another, pyramiding your experience if you don't like company practices. After a couple of jobs, however, you had better know what is going on within the company of your choice. You must be able to make each successive job or project more meaningful and each accomplishment more significant than the one before. Although this chapter emphasizes more short-term accomplishments in your beginning years, you will ultimately have to engage in some long hauls, participate in some larger team efforts, and engage in some longer, more complex activities in order to achieve greater responsibilities. Job jumpers always ultimately fail.

No company practices are perfect. Clearly, the successful DP professional will make sure he or she is engaged with good companies, is assigned meaningful projects, and achieves recognition.

Some companies recruit quickly. Some are so slow that they lose three waves of good applicants before they choose. They are waiting for the perfect applicant, who doesn't exist. When they find the candidate with the right qualifications, frequently the candidate is overpriced or will not do a repeat performance for money alone because he needs a different challenge for career purposes. The company does not want to train anyone. With the right prompting and good exposure, you could get a promotion. Companies are often more critical of their own, because they know you too well.

The search goes on. There are no perfect companies, jobs, or applicants. There are no perfect matches, but some are pretty close. When does the search end? When the company is tired of looking for the perfect one and gets realistic about the opening and what it takes to fill it. Remember that company personnel departments are under the gun to fill vacancies; this is their standard of performance. Emotion many times overrides logic in hiring or promoting from within.

They like you because of your human traits.

They believe you are intelligent by what you say and how you say it.

They think you are competent in data processing.

They can communicate with you.

They think you can and will help them with their work.

Your references will testify for you.

They simply need help.

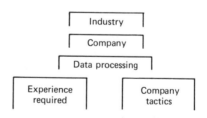

Remember, companies will often act independent of your opinion. Never place company loyalty above loyalty to yourself in the holy neurosis of competition.

Now you are in a position to plan your career.

Five
___

Create Your Own Future

OBJECTIVES AND GOALS

By this point you should be aware of the distinction between your objectives and goals. Your objectives refer to what you want from your whole career. Your goals refer to the intermediate steps along the way. Your career plan may encompass many objectives, for example:

To maximize your life earnings in data processing
To achieve continual growth in technical hardware and software knowledge
To outperform your competition
To achieve a national reputation
To own your own data processing business
To be a good technician and stay up to date

Your career plan may involve many intermediate goals, for example:

To achieve a position as senior programmer analyst this year
To attain data base software experience in the next six months
To become data processing manager with your current company this year
To manage the installation of a new financial system development project next year
To become the lead operator this year

Each goal must contribute to your longer-range objective. Planning is a primary prerequisite for success in your DP career.

Clearly, to achieve both goals and objectives you must acquire superior technical, social, and political skills. Most DP professionals concentrate on the technical and do very little about the latter two areas. It is critical for you to pay close attention to factors that can limit your progress. These may be lack of education, technical training, personal social skills, administration ability, or the lack of planning itself.

Alternatives exist in any career, and planning involves the selection of the course of action that best enables you to meet your goals. This action can mean many painful choices, such as long hours in evening schools, extra effort on the job, moving to another location, completing work in advanced areas, or participation in business activity projects that improve your visibility and communication skills. There is just so much time to plan, acquire, and act. Flexibility involves willingness to change your plans, detour, and keep moving toward your objectives, despite circumstances beyond your control. Your plan may fail, so continual adjustment is necessary. You have to keep your eyes open to all events and information that could cause your plan to fail. Your boss, your peers, your subordinates, company action, and changes in technology are examples of competitive factors that can effect your plan. Surprise can be your principle enemy. The simplest plan is frequently the best.

You should plan your objectives and associated goals in terms of a realistic time frame within which they can be achieved. Spending too long in any activity can effectively preclude moving from one position level to another. You may eventually earn too much for your span of experience. For example, you may earn too much as a computer operations supervisor to achieve a programming position. You may earn too much as a senior systems analyst to gain valuable computer operations management experience.

If you keep your goals before you at all times, you will be in a better position to make rational choices as job opportunities arise. It is important to remember that any radical departure from your initial DP career can cause serious setbacks. Two years managing your father's flower store or tarring roofs can be fatal. Continuity is a key to progress.

YOUR DETAIL RÉSUMÉ

Once you have determined your objectives and goals, you are ready to prepare your detail résumé. The detail résumé allows you to see all of the data processing activities and functions in which you have experience and to delineate all of those activities and functions in which you plan to engage.

Few DP professionals ever plan their careers as effectively as they perform their employer's work. Figure 5-1 is an organization format for your detail résumé.

Section I   Displays personal data.

Section II   Displays the industry and employer- company-related data.

Section III   Displays the detail activities and functions for every experience classification and level in which you have engaged or plan to engage.

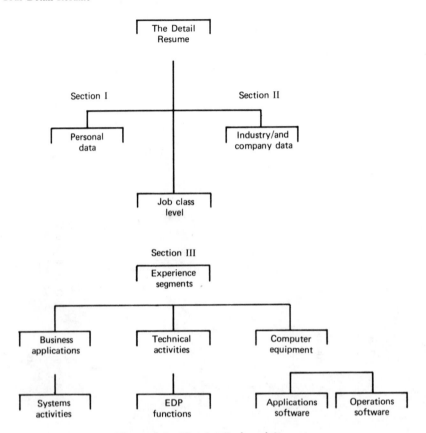

Figure 5-1   The detail résumé format.

The detail résumé format is designed to allow for multiple occurrences of companies and experiences within each company.

Each experience is displayed within the job level or class in which it occurred.

Systems activities usually occur within and relative to business applications.

Technical activities, EDP functions, and computer equipment experience may or may not be directly related to descrete business applications.

Certain segments under each job class/level may be blank.

You may question the need for detailing every job activity; however, every bit of experience can have a bearing on jobs you may subsequently hold. It is also clear that a small bit of experience in a given area may catch the eye of a potential employer and give you an edge over your competitor. The detail résumé is the basis for preparing your career plan and the all-

THE DETAIL RÉSUMÉ

I. Personal Data

NAME	Last: French	First: Mark				Middle: Nelson	

ADDRESS	312 Clover Lane, Louisville, Kentucky 40280

PERSONAL	Social Security No.	Birthdate	Married	Citizen	Number of	Class	Percent
	355-24-2121		Yes No	Yes No	Dependents		Travel
		12/29/61	x	x	3		10

	Telephone
	502-896-6329

Next Position

	Name		Level	Class
	Systems Manager, Planning		Senior	Systems

REFERENCES						
Name		Company		Position	Telephone	
1. JOHN MARLEY		University of Louisville		Professor	(502) 893-3304	
2. DON WOOD		Touche Ross, Inc.		Partner	(312) 589-6200	
3. JOHN GLEN		U.S. Senator		Ohio	(513) 812-5069	

EDUCATION					
Educational Institution	Field of Study	Degree	No. of Years	Year Degree Received	Average Grades
1. University of Illinois	Computer science	BS	4	1972	4/4
2. Northwestern University	Finance	MBA	2	1974	4/4
3. Wharton School of Finance	Economics	PHD	3	1977	4/4
4. Institute of Foreign Studies	Currency	LLB	1	1978	4/4

LICENSES, CERTIFICATION		
MEMBERSHIPS	1. CPA Illinois	3. A.I.C.P.A.
	2. Phi Beta Kappa	4. A.S.M.

OTHER INTERESTS	1. Republican Party State Chairman	3. Oriental languages
	2. Chamber of Commerce	4. Karate tournament

LOCATION PREFERENCE	Region	State	City
	1. MIDWEST	ILLINOIS	CHICAGO
	2. WEST	CALIFORNIA	SAN FRANCISCO
	3. EAST	MASS	BOSTON

II. Industry Company Data For Each Company

EMPLOYER

Company Name		**Address**
General Motors		11030 Greenvale Road, Detroit, Michigan

Industry
Automobile

Major product
Passenger cars

From	**To**	**Earnings/Year**	
1/78	1/81	21K start 28K end	5K bonus

REFERENCES

Name	**Position**	**Telephone**
1. Albert Montag	Sr. VP Finance	(312) 827-8968
2. Edward Haig	Controller	(312) 555-2200

Hired?
Management trainee

Terminated?
Management cutback

JOB MOVEMENTS
1. G.M. Training Institute (Manufacturing)
2. Computer Programming Simulation
3.
4.

TRAINING

MAJOR ACCOMPLISHMENTS (Begin each statement with an action verb)
1. Planned, designed, and programmed a plant inventory model
2. Designed a data collection system to cut production costs
3. Designed a financial currency system to accelerate foreign currency exchange
4. Wrote a financial simulator program to communicate various plant cost variances

III. Company Experience Data For Each Company Job

COMPANY General Motors

Job Title Senior Systems Analyst

Level	Class	From	To	People Supervised	Highest Salary	Highest Rating (1–10)
Supervisor	Analyst	1/80	1/81	2	$2330/month	10

	Occurrence I	**Occurrence II**	**Occurrence III**
EXPERIENCE BUSINESS APPLICATION	General Ledger	Financial	Accounts Payable
SYSTEMS ACTIVITIES	1. Forms design 2. Flowchart system 3. Establish financial controls	Create models Designed reports/displays Reviewed with management	Create exchange table Reviewed with I.R.S. Reviewed with management
TECHNICAL ACTIVITIES	1. Reset cost centers 2. Program specifications 3. Programmed	Program specifications Programmed Audited results	Program specifications Supervised programming Prepared base case
TECHNICAL OPERATIONS	1. — 2. — 3. —	Keyed data Operated computer	Supervised installation Supervised operation
COMPUTER EQUIPMENT	**Manufacturer** IBM **Model** 370/168	DEC PDP/11	IBM 370/168
APPLICATIONS SOFTWARE	**Vendor** IBM **Designation** COBOL-CICS	DEC ASSEM	IBM COBOL-IMS
OPERATING SOFTWARE	**Vendor** IBM **Designation** MVS	DEC RSTS/E	IBM MVS

important interview résumé. You may want to use the standard names of activities displayed in Tables 2-1, 3-2, and 3-3 to more efficiently describe your experience.

YOUR CAREER PLAN

Your detail résumé tells you what you have done and is the basis from which you can proceed. Without a career plan, you are simply looking at jobs. The random acceptance of jobs will lead to disastrous results in the long run. You will end up protecting what you have and waiting for the new boss to arrive to give you your next assignment, or to replace you with one of his associates.

One programmer with a computer science degree initially took a COBOL programming job, continued for four years, achieved a higher-than-standard rate of pay, and too late realized he could not utilize his quantitative analysis background without a significant pay reduction. The search for a company that would even consider him in quantitative analysis activities was complex. Personnel departments of various companies insisted that something must be wrong with him for him to consider a pay cut, and he had not programmed in FORTRAN or PL-1 for four years. The programmer persisted and found what he knew in the long run would meet his objectives, despite having wasted two years of his career.

Career planning begins with a look at your current detail résumé. It shows what you have done so far: where you are and what your next move should be. Logic and realism must prevail. If you are thirty-five years old and still going for a BS degree, there is no way you are going to be the data processing vice president for a major U.S. corporation. Variations of this example exist for all levels of the DP hierarchy. Some counseling with a top-notch DP placement agent or a successful DP pyramid head can give you a good perspective on jobs and the experience needed to acquire them.

You can make several observations from your own detail résumé. The first observation concerns your age and job class or level as it relates to earnings and experience. You may want to draw an earnings line on log paper to keep track of whether your earnings are increasing at an increasing or decreasing rate. Owing to inflation, you may find that you are earning relatively less, even though your take-home pay is increasing.

Are you repeating the same types of experience or are you actually involved in various activities and functions? Is your job level what it should be for your age? Is your pay commensurate with your position and experience? Naturally, there are limits to what you can be paid in any job class or level.

There are some positions in data processing that simply require certain training or education. Are you missing any of these necessary qualifications? Has new technology been introduced that is vital to your future? Are you promotable within your present company? Are you getting the breadth and depth of experience you need?

After completing a detail résumé for your present job, keep working on it. Add the experience which you believe you must have to meet your future objectives and each successive job. Next, prepare a set of sequential goals to complete each segment of your career plan. You will also need to specify those job levels and classes you have to hold to achieve each successive step. Equally important is the length of time you can remain in each job before you move up or out. Always let one phase of your career support those to come. Difficult? Yes. Impossible? No. Only the real winners will attempt, complete, and implement their own DP career plan. The losers will founder until only short-term gains can be achieved and it's time to hang it up and try to hang in at their present level of competence until they are overtaken by the next generation.

Figure 5-2 shows a sample career plan. It documents the person's growth from student to vice president of data processing within a major company environment.

Goals	Time (years)	Position Name	Action Goal
1	4	BS, computer science	Graduate and select the industry
2	1	Programmer trainee	Select the company/opportunity
3	1	Programmer, junior	Become proficient in COBOL
4A	1	Programmer, senior	Assembler, FORTRAN, PL-1 on major vendor hardware
4B	1	Programmer analyst	Learn at least two business applications/systems
5	1	Systems analyst	Perform systems development activities
6	1	Project leader	Supervise a systems development project
7	2	Manager systems/programming	Manage multiple systems and programming activities
8	2	Manager, computer operations	Manage all technical operations
9	2	Director, data processing planning	Manage all technical operations and planning
10	1	Vice president of information systems	Assume responsibility for all data processing developments and operations
Total	16 years		

Figure 5-2   A career plan to achieve pyramid head status

A career plan is much easier to create than to implement. Several job changes may be required if no opportunities exist within your own company as your career timetable limits are reached.

When your plan is completed, the best place to begin implementation is within your present company. You can improve your career from within if you make your requirements known properly. Your peers and your boss can either help you or be your competitors. You can achieve a good reputation if you communicate intelligence, motivation, likability, and cooperation. Forget about bad-mouthing certain company practices, your assignments, your boss, and incompetent users. Sometimes emotions overrule, but people are the same in all companies and you will need good references, if you leave—someone who can testify for you. Your boss is your best reference. Users and other company managers are good references. Do good things for users and coworkers. Don't let your ego get in the way of progress.

Frequently in the technical DP world, technology and intelligence conflict with human emotion. You may be absolutely right in a technical argument with your boss or peers, for example, regarding the best computer/ software. But if someone else, especially the boss, is already committed to another alternative and you push your idea, you lose. Timing is everything. There are no fast jumps up the pyramid through a single idea. If you try a long bomb or an end run on anyone, your probability of success is 1 percent. But if you fail you are assured that your advisary will never forget—you might as well pack your bags. Many superior DP professionals have difficulty with team efforts, because they are ahead of the pack. If you want to build your career, there is no substitute for compromise. The truly superior person allows others to win also, even if the technical solution is not the best.

Even the smallest tasks done well will display that you are a superstar person. Become known as a person who knows his job and works diligently. Complaints needlessly upset you and everyone around you. They accomplish nothing. Your personal contacts in other departments of the company are very important, because their statements to their bosses and your boss eventually end up working for or against you. Give your boss a stroke now and then. It's not to your advantage if he ever feels threatened by you. Self-discipline shows your capacity for leadership. Never have lunch alone. The more people you know at all levels of the company, the more you will learn about the total operations. Listen 80 percent of the time, talk 20 percent of the time. Never discuss personalities; others will do enough of that.

Some DP professionals believe that if their career is moving along they can cease looking for new opportunities. Wrong! You don't have to wait until you have experienced a setback or a slowdown to actively seek something better. In fact, the best time to effect a career move is when you are riding the crest of peak performance in your current job, just after a good review. Career opportunities appear in many places at the least expected times, frequently in a distant location. Opportunities often require personal sacrifice to gain needed experience at the right time, if career acceleration is to be achieved. Once you have decided to accelerate, your job search begins. If you can't make the decision to accelerate, you can forget about the rest of this book. If you are a decision maker, your interview résumé is the next step. Strangely enough, most DP professionals are not decision makers; consequently, only a few continue to advance. The majority will not move out of town; they expect the big opportunity to appear twenty miles from where they are currently living. Remember Chisolm's law: Anytime things appear to be going better, you have overlooked something.

YOUR INTERVIEW RÉSUMÉ

An interview résumé is designed to accomplish two things: (1) to get an interview with the company of your choice; (2) to get management to agree to approve an offer even if they have not interviewed you personally. You may think the résumé is not important. Wrong. Presentation and the use of key action words make the difference. The interview résumé highlights your most significant achievements. It compliments you personally and shows how you have progressed. It also shows how well you can write and communicate. The résumé sells your progress, stability, applications knowledge, systems activity, technical background, and hardware and software experience. Above all, your interview résumé positively displays those jobs you have completed, describes how they contributed to profits and cost saving or enhanced company operations. The completion of projects is the most important of all attributes in attaining another job. A senior executive of a major U.S. corporation once told me that the corporation's future leaders are chosen from among those who take the most insignificant task and complete it as though it were the most important job in the company.

You must be able to talk from your interview résumé (using your detail résumé data) as though you consider your work highly significant. If you don't value what you have done, no employer will value you, regardless of the technical proficiency you exhibit. One programmer had only worked minor maintenance jobs but succeeded in showing a potential employer how he was actually responsible for ongoing systems worth over a million dollars. He obtained a significant new position as manager of current systems enhancement.

Figure 5-3 is a sample basic interview résumé. It is sufficient to display your background and accomplishments. Your personal objectives should not appear on résumés, since they may conflict with those of the reader or his company's needs and preclude an interview opportunity for a job that would represent a good alternate goal, one that could change your plan. Personal hobbies and leisure activities are not critical to the résumé. Professional activities do belong there.

The major sections of the basic interview résumé are:

Personal data
Education and special qualifications
Industry
Company
Business applications
Systems and programming activities
EDP functions
Hardware and software experience
Summary

Many books have been written describing the most successful résumés. Many of these reflect some interesting gimmicks and tricks described by so-called experts in the field of job hunting. Data processing professionals do not need any cool or unusual résumés. The DP professionals who are going to interview you are seasoned veterans, who for the most part have come up through the ranks. They will quickly detect any exaggerations concerning your battle ribbons. What counts is your experience and what you can really do. The DP management nature is less influenced by humor, claims, and punch lines than other company management. "Accurate," "factual," "precise," "concise" and "action-oriented" describe the best résumés.

The basic résumé (Figure 5-3) gives a minimum amount of detail about the DP professional. The basic résumé is geared to accomplishment, knowledge, and experience. Other DP résumés are embellishments of these basics.

The basic résumé sequence is in the order of importance in the DP job world as you increase your position level. For example, industry experience is more important than specific computer hardware knowledge at the systems manager level.

Personal Data

Consider your name. The common statement of your name should be straightforward. Clearly, "Mark French" is better than any of the following for obvious reasons.

M. Nelson French   M. "Bud" French
M. N. French   M. French

MARK FRENCH

Personal Data

312 Clover Lane   No dates
Louisville,   Married, two children
Kentucky 40280   Omit earnings
(502) 896-6329   Omit physical descriptions
                         Omit religious affiliation
                         Omit photos
                         Omit references
                         Omit age
                         Omit military service

Education/Special Qualifications

School	Degree	Major
University of Illinois	BS	Computer Science/Accounting (Highest Honors)
Northwestern University	MBA	Qualitative Analysis (Summa Cum Laude)
Certified Public Accountant	CPA	Illinois

Industry Experience

Manufacturing, 2 years
Distribution, 3 years   Omit reason for terminations

Company	Period	Product
Cincinnati Gear, Inc.	1979–81	Machine tools
General Motors Corp.	1976–79	Engines

Business Applications

Bill of material	Accounts payable	Warehouse
Production scheduling	Accounts receivable	General ledger
Inventory control	Purchasing	Financial planning
Fixed-asset control	Property acquisition	Bank loans
	System audits	

Figure 5-3   A basic interview résumé

Put your name on all pages of the résumé and number the pages.

Your address is important because it reflects where you are relative to the company. If you are in Louisville applying for a position in Seattle, your counterpart in Seattle will get preference, owing to interview and moving costs, all other factors being equal. If your mother lives in Seattle and you have living quarters there, using her address at least displays your connection with the location. Companies often believe that hiring a person from a faraway location can be more risky in terms of staying power. If you have some preference for the location of the company, say why; it helps to show

Systems and Programming Activity

Job Class Level	Activity
Project Leader	Implemented a new financial system
Systems Analyst	Developed an on-line manufacturing data base system
Systems Analyst	Optimized a cash investment system
Programmer Analyst	Developed and programmed a warehouse scheduling system
Programmer	Programmed a manufacturing data collection system
Programmer	Programmed a fixed-asset control system
Programmer	Modified an accounts receivable system

Hardware/Software Experience

Vendor/Equipment	Operating Software	Application Software	Years
IBM/370/158	OS/VSI	Cobol/CICS/PL-1	3
DEC PDP/11		Assembler	2
IBM System 3	CCP	RPG II	1
MSA		General Ledger	1
AIC		Payroll	1
IBM		MRP, CAD, CAM	2

Summary

Comprehensive experience in manufacturing and financial analysis. Will consider relocation for a management position with good potential in Midwest or South. Will travel to 15 percent. Excellent communication skills, performance rating, and references.

Note: The strict chronological sequence of experience is not displayed because time is never a measure of depth and quality of experience.

Figure 5-3 (Continued)

local attachment. If there is none, "I always wanted to see the Pacific Ocean" is not appropriate. Certain things should be omitted from a résumé. Consider the following:

1 Don't date the résumé. You may want to use it for a longer period of time, and someone may wonder whether you are still available.
2 Indication of being married and having children shows stability. Do not give your children's names.
3 Do not indicate earnings. The opportunity may be worth less than you are earning now. You may be near the top of their salary range and you could be passed over if they assume your price is too high. Get the interview and you may get a chance to prove you are worth a lot more to the company. They may raise their range after they talk to you.
4 Omit physical descriptions. You are not applying for Mr. or Miss America

contest. Racial references are not appropriate. You do not need to comment on your health.

5   Omit religious or political affiliations. Generally, holy wars are illegal. If the organization is packed with your denomination, it's okay to let them know you belong. Hobbies, interests, and extracurricular activities do not add to your value. A company may not care what you do in your spare time. If it does, they will find out at the interview what your spare-time activities are.

6   Omit photographs. Some hiring companies may prefer females. You are not applying for an actor's position.

7   Omit references. These come after the interview and usually just before an offer is made.

8   Do not state your age. Some old-timers are still pretty good and some youngsters have more on the ball than some supposedly experienced types.

9   Don't mention military service unless it applies directly to the total business experience. "Mess cook for two years" does not promote the DP image. Military computer school does.

Education and Special Qualifications

1   Include all of your formal education above high school. Include name of education institution, and your majors and minors.

2   Include all specialized degrees, certificates, and honors received, but do not date them.

3   CDP and CCP are still important certificates.

4   If you have no formal training, emphasize that you are a self-made man or woman. There are still many who value those who have clawed their way up the pyramid. Don't try to hide a lack of formal schooling. Turn the adversity into the advantage of being a mustang.

5   Include some of the more important software training courses you have taken, but not all.

6   Include professional and business-related affiliations.

7   Mentioning honors and business awards is appropriate.

Experience

1   Indicate the industry you have specialized in and the length of time you have spent in it. If the company is in a related field they will value this knowledge.

2   Give your company name, your length of service, and the company's

product. You may describe the company if you do not name it, owing to confidentiality (e.g., a large oil company). No addresses or supervisors names, please. No reasons for leaving should be given.

3 The basic résumé shows all of the business applications you know, regardless of where you learned them or how long you spent on each. Breadth of experience shows up in the basic résumé.

4 Accomplishments and activities at each job level show up in the basic résumé, regardless of the company or how long it took. Remember to state what you did, why you did it, and what benefit accrued to the company because of your work.

5 Hardware and software technical experience listed in the basic résumé should clearly indicate vendor/computer equipment model, operating software, applications software, and number of years you have been exposed to it. The exposure period may only have been part time, but it should be in-depth exposure.

6 The summary should describe your position on relocation and travel and your personal communication skills, including reference to your past performance as appraised by employers.

7 Chronological completeness, accuracy, and correct spelling still count.

There are two other modified types of DP résumés you can construct from your basic résumé for different emphasis.

A chronological emphasis
A job class emphasis

It can be to your advantage to construct these alternate résumé types, because of the position for which you are applying or to offset certain deficiencies you may have. Planning these varied résumés will help you to remember your career plan, strengths, and weaknesses, so that you will not get caught short at the interview or end up taking the wrong job.

The *chronological-type résumé* is used when you want to emphasize and detail your length of service, your increase in responsibility (job levels), and your position titles. You should include a few sentences on what, why, and how you performed the activities on the position. If a chronological sequence shows high performance, use it (see Figure 5-4)

The *job/class-type* résumé (Figure 5-5) is used when you want to expand on the accomplishments mentioned in the chronological-type résumé; when your length of service at companies has not been long and so you have not achieved progression in positions of increased responsibility; or when your experience has been at considerable depth in certain business applications, systems activities, technical activities, or computer hardware and software.

When you want to emphasize depth knowledge, use the job class-type résumé. You simply describe your levels of experience in short sentences, then list the companies and dates of employment at the end of the résumé.

The interview résumé tells just enough to require the recruiting company to ask some questions: of course they need more detail—to fail to interview you may lead to their losing a good employee. They know they must offer you more money than you currently earn, but your salary goal is not on the résumé. (Salary negotiation is actually accomplished after the first interview.)

Many items are purposely omitted from the interview résumé. Amount of time spent in the various applications areas is omitted because it is seldom a measure of the competence and knowledge gained. A DP professional can learn more in six months on a systems project than the operational staff learns in six years, because the former is not restricted to a section of the total operation and because his or her experience may be very broad.

Personnel departments often count years, not depth of experience. Don't do a memory dump in your résumé. There may be many jobs available in a company other than the one advertised. Insist that you are qualified for many positions. You will get to talk to more people and learn about the company from many points of view. Remember, résumés don't get jobs, and you are seldom hired for a new position because of your experience alone. You will be hired when you display you are intelligent, competent, motivated, personable, and knowledgeable. These qualities can only be displayed in the interview, not on paper. Decline to complete a detailed employment application until after the first interview, but take any test they want to throw at you. One programmer analyst volunteered to write a program for the company on the spot. Hiring can be a highly emotional experience for both the employer and the applicant.

THE USE OF WORDS

How you use words is extremely important. Use complete statements. Begin with action verbs wherever possible to describe what you did. Some words are weaker than others. Consider the following word pairs. Which word shows a stronger positive contribution?

implemented	vs.	administered
programmed	vs.	reviewed
created	vs.	improved
established	vs.	audited
directed	vs.	influenced

generated	vs.	participated
streamlined	vs.	improved
strengthened	vs.	revised
sold	vs.	recommended
lead	vs.	conducted

Your words indicate whether you are an active or passive personality and show your communication skills. Every one is subject to advertising, and your résumé is your selling tool. Adjectives help—if you use them discreetly.

Consider using the following words to describe you and your work in your résumé.

efficient	enthusiastic	systematic
energetic	logical	tactful
alert	loyal	hardworking
dependable	reliable	conscientious
disciplined	self-reliant	active

And remember:

Use 8½ x 11 white bond paper.

Type neatly.

Limit yourself to two pages.

Correct spelling and grammer reflect well on you.

COBOL is still spelled COBOL.

Drop unnecessary words.

Avoid use of first person ("I").

Figure 5-4 is a chronological interview résumé and is an expansion of the basic résumé. Note that the résumé shows the following:

1 The job candidate has an appropriate education from recognized schools.
2 The time in jobs is sufficient to allow considerable growth in career and business knowledge. The person is not a job jumper, and has good length of service.
3 Each job builds toward the next. He plans his moves.
4 Accomplishments abound; the candidate knows what was accomplished by his work and why.
5 Good steady job level progression identifies him as a fast-track individual. He does not have one year of experience, five times.

MARK FRENCH

Personal Data

2108 Montana Ave.   Married, 2 children
Cincinnati, Ohio 45211   (513) 896-6329

Education

School

BS   University of Illinois   Computer science/accounting (highest honors)
MBA   Northwestern University   Qualitative analysis (summa cum laude)
CPA   Certified public accountant
       Illinois
Member of Mensa, 1980

1979–   Manager, Special Projects, Cincinnati Gear, Inc.
PRESENT   A Corporation manufacturing high-precision tools.

Responsible for control and enhancement of the entire financial system, including cost, budgets, statements, accounts receivable/payable, payroll, fixed assets, and simulated projections. Utilized MRP, CAD, CAM concepts.

Implemented a new financial system to simulate the total effect of individual orders on the bottom-line profit of the firm, resulting in the acceptance of only high-profit orders. Utilized MSA, AIC, and PL-1 software packages.

Promoted from systems analyst to manager.

Designed, programmed, and implemented an on-line manufacturing data base for tool products resulting in reduced costs and better decision making. DEC PDP/11 assembler.

Designed and programmed an automated cash investment system to optimize the cash flow of investment in purchased-parts inventory, resulting in a large savings of inventory carrying cost.

Figure 5-4 A chronological interview résumé

6 The candidate knows how to communicate.

7 There are several positions for which he can qualify (i.e., director, DP or finance, controller)

Figure 5-5 is a job class interview résumé. It is an expansion of the basic résumé emphasizing DP activities and functions. This type of résumé is frequently used by operations and technical support specialists, where specific experience is the key to the next job. The résumé shows the following:

1 The candidate has appropriate formal education from good schools.

2 His average job tenure is 3 years, all in a wide-range technical area.

1976–1978   Programmer analyst, General Motors Corporation.

A corporation division manufacturing automobile engines.

Developed and programmed a warehouse scheduling system resulting in lower inventory costs and better scheduling techniques.

1978, promoted from programmer to programmer analyst.

Programmed and implemented a factory data-collection system resulting in a speedup of engine assemblies and better quality control of scrap rates. IBM system 3, RPG II.

Programmed a fixed-asset control system to control machine maintenance, repairs, and depreciation, resulting in overall lower manufacturing costs.

Modified an interdivision billing system to more quickly display lags in purchased transferable parts among G.M. Divisions, resulting in more efficient part transfers.

Trained as a programmer on IBM 370/158 MVS using COBOL, CICS, CMS.

SUMMARY

Comprehensive experience in manufacturing and related financial analysis. Will consider relocation for a management position with good potential in Midwest or South. Will travel 15 percent. Excellent communication skills, performance ratings, and references.

Figure 5-4   (Continued)

3   He is very adaptable to a wide range of technical activities.

4   He knows how to communicate precisely.

5   All of his experience has probably been as an individual contributor, but he wants management responsibility.

6   He rates an interview.

THE JOB SEARCH

Many DP professionals begin their job search by mailing their interview résumé to every job advertisement or company with a job title that seems relevant. Only a small percentage are good jobs or result in a response or an interview, and this practice exposes you to every secretary in town. Your résumé is filed and forgotten because no job is available at that time. And it simply costs too much for a company to follow up on résumés after a month, because by that time most applicants are long gone. Some DP professionals use personal contacts at other companies, but it is difficult to attain a higher job level unless you know someone at a high level.

The most effective individual search can be accomplished by first

ROGER TEXPERT

PERSONAL DATA

2108 N. Syndrome Drive   Married
Cincinnati, Ohio 45228   (513) 471-8182

EDUCATION

B.S. University of Chicago   Electrical Engineering (honors)
M.S. ' University of Chicago   Computer Sciences (highest honors)

COMPUTER PROGRAMMING PROFICIENCY

COBOL   FORTRAN
Assembler   Pascal

Have written over 500 major application programs using the above languages over a 5-year period.

SPECIALIZED SOFTWARE PROGRAMMING

CICS Made modifications to CICS internal code to increase efficiencies in line loading. Proficient at macro and command level.

IMS DL-1 Designed logical and physical data bases to improve DB/DC access efficiency. Wrote specialized DP file access routines.

TOTAL Adapted total data base software to minicomputer technology for two vendors.

OS/VS/MVS Performed system generations and modified software to ease conversion to on line environments.

Figure 5-5 A job class interview résumé

selecting a location and a company you have researched effectively. Then you must make a contact with the top DP management person or his boss. Don't be embarrassed to call on the telephone. You can say simply, "Please connect me with data processing." Usually the switchboard operator rings you right through. Don't ask her who the DP manager is—the switchboard operator may be instructed to ring the personnel department for all personnel inquiries. Your telephone conversation may run approximately as follows:

"Is this the DP manager? . . . No? . . . May I speak to him please,"
"May I tell him who is calling?"
"Yes, a programmer,"
"May I give him your name?"
"Yes, John Jones. What is his name?"
"Jim Davis, but he's in a meeting."
"Please have Mr. Davis call me at 882-6969? Thank you."

Communications Designed and programmed a data communication network utilizing Bi/syncronous techniques to tie Burroughs and IBM endpoint computers to a centralized corporate data base.

Design Participated in hardware design and software programming to optimize I/O driver efficiency and improve com line/disk access utilization.

Consulting Acted as a software consultant to computer hardware vendors and major corporations in improving computerized operating efficiencies.

Good working knowledge of the following:

Hardware: IBM 370, 4431, 4341, System 1
            Burroughs B7800
            Amdahl 470/V8
            Univac 1100 Series

Software: OS, VS, MVS, DOS/VSE
            MCP, CICS, IMS, TOTAL, DMS, IDMS, CMS
            ENVIRON/1, NOMAD, RAMIS, VANDL/1

EMPLOYMENT

Cincom Systems, Inc.   Technical specialist   1979-81
IBM Corporation   Senior technical programmer   1976-79
M.S.A., Inc.   Technical support representative   1973-76

SUMMARY

Comprehensive experience in technical software activities. Will consider relocation for a management position with good potential on West Coast. Will travel 40 percent. Excellent communication skills, performance reviews, and references.

Figure 5-5 (Continued)

Tell the DP pyramid head that you have heard he is one of the best at his job and you simply want to *meet* him to get some advice. He will be flattered, unless he is a computer. The DP pyramid head can evaluate you for many positions in his own company, even though you eventually may have to go through the personnel department. If a position does not exist, he often may refer you to his counterpart in another company with whom you can have lunch the next day. If it is only a lunch and not a job interview, you will learn more than you expected. Advice is free and yours for the asking. You may have to be persistent, but it pays off handsomely and you improve your interviewing skills significantly. Be sure to leave your interview résumé, because he may soon have a contact somewhere for you. Also, he sees many résumés from agencies and knows some companies that have recently lost people. He may be registered with an agency and know of companies with jobs on the basis of his own interviews. It works, try it

—and be sure you are prepared with some excellent questions in a structured format so that the conversation never lags.

There is no substitute for knowing top DP people. Join your local DPMA (Data Processing Management Association) or ACM (Association for Computing Machinery) professional groups and attend the meetings. This activity can tell you about industries, companies, business activities, and your ability to compete. It is also a place to meet people who can help you if you subtly let it be known what your next job should be, what you do, and what company you are with.

There are many ways to find jobs, but the real career positions are difficult to find and harder to get. The search can be very time-consuming because you must be in the right place just when they need you most and have the right qualifications to trade for your own new experience needs. The search can take months. Fortunately, most of us are human. We deviate from our plan, if we ever had one. A good selling job by a headhunter, a little more responsibility, a good title, sunny Florida, or some more cash, and we are off and running. Even one of these factors may do it. Some candidates have even been convinced to take pay cuts for the thrill of working for some companies in the Sunbelt. Somehow the grass can seem greener on the other side. Frequently it is more yellow, but they never tell you that ahead of time. Research is your only protection against losing companies, losing assignments, dumb DP management, and disinterested company management.

Your research must provide answers to some of the following questions:

Is the industry in a growth phase?

Is the company experiencing high earnings?

What is the company's financial position?

Is the company a leader or a follower? Are its products A-1?

Will working for the company improve your résumé?

Are the company's products something you can get interested in? After all, you are going to be assisting the company's marketing, engineering, operations, and accounting departments.

How is a downslide economy likely to affect the company? An upturn? If the company is in a weak position, DP staff will be terminated.

You can get all of this information simply by asking people who work there. You can get a stockbroker's report, the annual report, or take a look at several reports by independent research companies.

By now you are probably asking, "Is it worth all this." It certainly is. If you get into the wrong situation and want out, you have jeopardized your career progress. One candidate took a job with a major trucking firm as a DP director knowing things were a little shaky. Murphy's law "If it *can* go wrong, it *will* go wrong" went into effect. The banks called the notes, the company declared bankruptcy, and he was out looking again after three months with a new title, competing against those with considerably more time at the DP director job level. He had to step back to a systems and programming manager position and will have to explain this blunder for the rest of his career. He could have avoided this problem by proper research and caution.

One effective way to search for a position is to develop friends who are a couple of levels higher than you, perhaps who have moved around quite a bit. Even vendor representatives can be helpful in identifying the good DP shops and managers. Always ask where the turnover is high and, conversely, where the DP staff quality is superior.

Don't be afraid to call a couple of members of any staff at home. Find out how it really is. One person on the staff of a large company told a candidate how bigness had narrowed her career from the start. She had been given a high rate of pay but had spent two years working on programs she knew little about. In her early years, the technical training had been excellent, but after that, the company forgot about job rotation and promotion. Company reviews were good, but for four years she was evaluated solely on how efficiently her code executed.

Another candidate heard of an opening from a friend who had just left a medium-size manufacturer. Upon investigating the company, he found out that pressure and work had been so great that one of the computer operations staff had attempted suicide when his job was threatened.

One successful candidate had been considering a small company for over a year simply because his brother had worked there eight years before. Upon reading in the newspaper that the company had acquired another plant in North Carolina, he dropped in to visit his brother's friend. He was introduced to the VP of finance and was offered the DP manager job the next day. His curiosity and background were not planned carefully but were timed right.

Yet another candidate heard that a certain smaller shop with minor vendor's hardware was really screwed up. He called the president and told him of his work in improving operations through better documentation and training. He was interviewed, given a six-month consulting contract, and was subsequently hired as DP director on the basis of his improvements.

In all of these and many more instances, the job search was based on various degrees of search and research of the company and its situation. Sometimes the opening does not exist until the right person walks in or exhibits interest in what is happening.

Another source of position opportunities is the companies' audit firm. The CPA firm often makes recommendations for the removal of some individuals from DP positions in order to strengthen their own DP control or to get their own hand in the pie. It is to your benefit to find out which CPA firm audits the books of your favorite company. Go visit the auditor, give him your résumé. He will keep his eye open for you. Frequently the auditors are asked whether they know of anyone who can help the company fix some of the problems they have identified (or in some instances invented). An auditor's recommendation gives you an automatic three points before the interview. If you are good, he may hire you on his staff for a while to get some added billing before placing you for a fee with his client (of course). After all, having one of his boys in the house helps him keep abreast of what's going on at all times.

Remember, research is the key. The following reference sources may help:

Thomas Register of American Manufacturers
Thomas Register Catalog File
Macmillan Job Guide to American Corporations
25,000 Leading U.S. Corporations
Standard and Poor's Register of Corporations, Directors, and Executives
Moody's Industrial Manual
Wall Street Journal
Business Week
Fortune

Only the bold will attempt and succeed in this vital search activity.

You may have noted that so far I have not emphasized responses to advertisements, letter writing, or using school alumni associations, simply because it is my opinion that these methods are not as effective as planning your next position and actively seeking it by personal contact and the telephone. Your résumé can be used after contact is established and you know whom you are dealing with.

Open advertisements such as those shown in Chapter 4 can be used to identify companies that are actively hiring DP professionals and agencies that are very active in the DP area. By law, an agency, CPA firm, or search firm must have a legitimate company job order for any position they advertise. Some do not; they misrepresent.

Study the sample advertisements in Chapter 4 and see if you would respond to any of them. It is clear that none of the ads tells you whether the job really fits the next step in your career plan. Many adjectives that are supposed to turn you on prevail, ranging from locations to keyword challenges. Don't get caught by Madison Avenue phrases. Before you respond, research the firm, ask questions, find out who's who. Then go directly to the individual you have been able to contact by phone. Ask him to review your résumé with the right person. Generally he will respond more quickly than a personnel department's internal mail system, some of which take weeks.

Your Use of Agencies

Good DP agencies flourish because they are on top of the job market. They know companies and people. They can quickly match good people to jobs. They maintain a high level of confidentiality. Good companies pay high fees to find quality people.

It simply saves time, effort, and money to work through an agency. Many DP professionals are always registered with a specialized DP agent but are never "actively looking for a job." Good DP personnel agents often know of upcoming openings in one company because they are about to place one of that company's employees with another company.

In the long run, companies know that a good agency probably has access to a greater number of higher quality applicants at any one time than their own ads could attract. Good jobs are frequently missed by qualified applicants because

Applicants are too busy to follow advertisements.

The timing is not right for an interview.

The job stays open longer than the ads run.

Ads are misleading and sometimes inaccurate.

Applicants don't have up-to-date résumés and don't have time or the facilities to answer a multitude of ads.

Applicants hesitate to risk identifying themselves.

Applicants do not know anything about the company.

It is often convenient for you to establish your goal requirement with a good DP agent and let him keep you advised of all the job openings for which you may qualify. Call him frequently; it's free.

Agency Activities

Data Processing agents are continuously screening DP job openings. They give advice to companies regarding job descriptions and salary levels required. Good DP agents advertise for good DP applicants for specific jobs and for their "opportunity" file. They match job opportunities and available applicants on a daily basis.

Companies and their job openings are promoted to all available qualified applicants. Applicants and their backgrounds are promoted with all companies that have "right now" and "future" openings.

The good DP agent sets up interviews and coaches both you and the company on what to expect during the interview. A good agent sells your qualifications to the company and will often get involved in salary negotiations. Many DP professionals create a barrier by setting their salary requirements too high to get even a screening interview on the telephone. Instead of investigating the career job opportunity, the DP professional will give the impression he is only concerned with money, and the company is immediately turned off. A good DP agent prevents this because of his experience in negotiating salary levels for the applicant and himself. He knows salaries should never be discussed at the first interview.

The DP professional is often not aware of the subleties of getting a job. Often he believes his experience will get him the best offer. It won't, but his ego cannot be shaken because he is an expert in his field and is confident that is enough.

As in any major transaction, an awareness of the phases of negotiation can mean a major difference in dollars and benefits in the final offer. Most companies are experts in negotiations and most DP applicants are not. A good DP agent follows a detailed checklist to get the best offer for the applicant on items you have never thought of. The agent wants the best offer too, because frequently his fee is dependent on the dollar amount of the offer. If he has been a successful agent for a long time, he can do the job much better than you, so why not let him use his talent for you.

Selecting an Agent

You must meet your agent. He should be a reputable DP professional and have actually held the kinds of jobs you will want to hold during your career. His knowledge of data processing, job classes, systems development, and hardware and software are critical when he presents you to companies. His credibility is an extension of you. He must be able to converse at the level of the DP executive. Your agent will sell part of his background when he speaks for you. If he doesn't understand data processing he can make you look like an amateur, and he won't be able to match you to a job. If his DP reputation is at stake, he will work for you and often compensate for some of your deficiences by emphasizing your strengths at the opportune moment. His opinion will be valued by the company. Your agent must be honest, thorough, persistent, motivated, intelligent, competent, and a DP professional.

The size of the agency you select is important. A national agent has access to job openings through his peers in other cities. Local, one-man offices simply can't compete with national DP agencies. The large agency will have all of the standing orders from national companies and specific job orders that have unique qualification requirements. Companies prefer a large assortment of applicants, which major agencies can provide, and you will never have to pay a fee with a good agency. The client companies agree to pay such fees.

The better your agent, the better your next job can be. Good agencies don't boiler-plate résumés and send them to every company in town. Poor agencies do this. If you work with them, you expose yourself needlessly: word soon gets out that you are looking; your own company may receive your résumé through a company friend, put you on the lost list, stop pay increases or promotions, or put you in line for termination at the first opportunity. You will never know what hit you. Check with various companies as to which agents are good, bad, or pushy. Call a few good companies and simply ask them, if they were to use a DP agent in town which would it be? The personnel department will tell you. Avoid the rest. This question may also get you an interview with the company. Never let an agent show you or send you on just a job interview. Insist that he tells you about the company and the job he wants you to interview for and why it fits your next career step.

Agent Relationships

Stay with one agent unless you are dissatisfied with his or her performance. If you are not satisfied with your own job search, your agent is your most important contact. You will have to register, completing his file data requirements. Some believe that five agents are better than one. Wrong. If you are an exclusive, the agent works harder for you.

Good DP agents will always prepare you for your job search. They will insist on a good résumé, give you a good résumé format, and evaluate your salary potential. They will listen carefully to your career requirements and give you an honest opinion of your potential and deficiencies. They will stay in touch with you by phone and pull no punches, even if it damages your ego. Data processing professional egos are so sensitive. A good DP agent will not send you on wild goose chases, which invite competition with other agencies for you. He or she may want to know what companies you have already talked to, what offers you have received, if any, and what other agencies are involved. Answer these questions, so your agent can spend time only on new situations for you. There can be absolutely no secrets between you and your agent. The effective agent who learns you have withheld information will drop you for hedging. If you are overexposed it's only a matter of time before placing you becomes impossible. If a poor agency has not marketed you well, even a good agent cannot help later. He cannot charge a fee if you have already been presented to the company.

If you have a few bad situations or references in your background, let your agent know so he won't get caught short at a critical point in his presentation of you to a company. He can support you if he knows. He will check out your references himself to be sure. Finagle's Law: Once a job is fouled up, anything done to improve it makes it worse.

A good agent will get you interviews for jobs that fit your requirements and career progression. This is his main objective. A good agent will maintain strict confidentiality. But don't tell even your best friend about a job, as he may get it before you do. People talk to each other, and it's a small, small world. If your friend interviews, he will be asked about you and may mention something that could kill your offer.

Stay employed at all costs. Jobs are always harder to get if you are unemployed, and employers may take advantage of your situation. It is human nature.

If you go on a couple of interviews and your agent is not calling you with feedback from the company viewpoint, he is not doing his job. Each interview must have feedback to improve your marketability. It may also help you to know yourself better. Your agent must be able to tell you why you did not get an offer. If you are overpriced, he will give you his opinion. Good agents always inform you whom they have contacted and why they could not get you an interview, so that no duplication will exist. He will always get your permission to send your résumé, and you should never get a call from a company out of the blue without a good briefing from him.

If your agent stays in touch with you, even without having set up an interview, the chances are he is on the lookout for you on a continuous basis. A good agent will not send you on an interview for a lateral move where there is no new type of experience to be gained. If he does it once, tell him not to. If he does it again, drop him quickly.

If you have an interview and do not get an acceptable offer, and if you don't know why, your agent has failed you. If your agent has not coached you in interviewing for the job, you are not dealing with a professional. Good agents prefer to market their own people locally. If you are seeking employment in another town, call or go to the agency in that town. They won't have to split commissions and will try harder.

Finally, good agencies know of job openings now, how long the company has been looking, and the salary range. Typically, the agent does not want to tell you the salary range because he knows you believe you should have the top of the range. He knows that many good jobs are passed up because of dickering over $500 one way or the other. He also knows that he can assist in raising the initial dollar offer, if everyone agrees that you are the person for the job.

The main purpose of the agent is to set up interviews for jobs for which you can qualify and which will further your career. However, he can be a significant third party in negotiating salary, shoring up weak areas, and getting added benefits. Many agencies will produce salary surveys and other statistics, but they are meaningless to you and what you are capable of getting. General guidelines should never be used in your specific case.

Some common reasons why your agent cannot get you an interview are:

You have no degree or proper educational credentials.

Your earnings are too high for your skill level.

You are short on technical experience.

You are short on business applications experience.

You and the interviewer would not have a good personality match.

You have had too many job changes.

No openings exist at the moment.

You have poor oral and written communication skills.

Your background and experience are a poor match for the jobs available.

You are overqualified for the job available.

You are not willing to move to a new location.

You cannot be contacted or go on interviews as required.

Your career progress has been too slow, indicating a lack of ability or ambition.

Some DP personnel believe they can use an agent to get them some interviews and a good offer, and then use that offer to get an increase at their present company. Be careful not to use an agent in this way. After expending that much effort, the aggressive agent will most certainly find your replacement at a lower salary and sell your current employer on replacing you. After all, you have used him; now he will use your disloyalty simply by stating he thought you were looking for a job and that your company may have an opening.

If you are content at your own company, be very careful about just taking a look or going on an interview. Some unethical agents arrange a one-time interview for you, then let your employer know you are there while they sell your replacement. Then they have got you. Be sure you are dealing with a top-grade confidential agent. Some companies immediately terminate a person they find looking for another job.

Above all, remember: An agent may want the best job for you, but don't let his or her enthusiasm to make a placement cause you to make a mistake.

SUMMARY

The aim of this chapter is to help explain the importance of planning your career positions and to present some tactics for getting interviews for those positions.

So far, we have examined the importance of the industry, the company, data processing organizations, types of experience, company behavior, the need for planning your career, and how to seek out positions that can help your career. All of these elements are important steps, but the most important single element in your repertoire is your ability to pass the interview. Some people less qualified than you get the job you should have. Why? You have learned your job, prepared your plan and résumés, and researched the company. Clearly, you should be ahead of your competition.

Six

Prepare Yourself to Get the Best Job

THE INTERVIEW

Up to this point, your activity has been directed toward obtaining an interview with a good company. The actual interview is strictly your responsibility. Your résumé, job experience, agent, or references cannot substitute for this crucial meeting. Because you are not often interviewed, it may be your weak point. Since the interviewer may interview frequently, it is one of his strong points. You are already at a disadvantage. On the other hand, you are a DP professional and probably have more knowledge of your field than the interviewer. It is wiser to stick with what you know. If you offer opinions in other areas, they may conflict with those of the interviewer (who may be quite knowledgeable), and you will create a poor impression.

Interview psychology is a long-neglected science. Like an athletic event, however, the athlete must be up to win an offer. When you are in a mood of tension, depression, anger, fatigue, or confusion, you lose. We all have psychological profiles that can change at various times, depending on our personal circumstances. One day you may be just the right person for the interview. On another day, you may be psychologically out of it and lose a real opportunity. You must be certain you are in proper physical and mental condition to engage with your potential employers. You must also consider the same psychological characteristics of the interviewers. You should be quick to observe the mood of those who are hiring. If either party is not ready, you should always reschedule the interview.

You must believe in yourself, have a high confidence level, and want to do well, or you most certainly will not. Nothing must interfere with your concentration at the interview time. Psychologically, many DP persons are so oriented toward precision that they forget their learning strengths and answer questions hesitatingly, in an attempt to be both truthful and precise with regard to their skills. Some interviewers equate this precision with weakness. The most qualified candidate seldom gets the job.

Your personal presentation is the key to a successful interview. When you are eyeball-to-eyeball, your ability to respond quickly to questions in an organized and consistent way could make the difference between success and failure. The first three minutes of the interview will set the tone and establish the necessary personal chemistry between you and the interviewer. Every body motion, eye movement, and facial expression is important. It is a human emotional encounter, after all. If you can act and feel as if you are already employed, the interview generally goes well. You have to know when to hold your cards, when to play, fold, or walk away.

Typically there are two types of interviews and four stages in the total process.

① The review of your job qualifications
② The survey of your personal characteristics
③ Your review of the company and its position
④ Mutual interaction

The screening interview deals primarily with stage 1. The company representative is simply trying to determine whether your background qualifies you for the position. Of course, stage 2 often becomes a factor in the screening process. Don't be surprised if this interview is short and sweet.

The in-depth type interview will involve all four stages, and generally you interview three persons, the personnel department representative (stage 1) your potential boss, and either his boss or a peer (stages 2, 3, and 4).

Sometimes its one on one, but other times its two or three on one over lunch. The stages are never clear-cut, so it is necessary to know exactly what is happening in the complete process. Awareness is the key.

The art of passing the interview is an entirely different talent than performing the job. Few DP professionals consider the difference carefully enough. Because DP persons are in high demand, frequently the attitude is "My résumé speaks for itself"—stage 1 is all that counts. Wrong! In all DP jobs of any substance, your competition is also in the running, and in fact they may have as strong or stronger DP background than you.

In any interview it is important for you to consider your job strengths and weaknesses. You may be interviewing for (1) a lateral opportunity, in the same job class or level; (2) a promotional job level opportunity, or (3) a change in job class. You must discover up front what job class or level position you are interviewing for.

Your competitors will be in these same competitive categories. Clearly, if you are in category 1 and your competition is in categories 2 or 3, you have the advantage. The converse is also true, providing your salary requirements are essentially the same.

In the area of job experience, competition is where the detail résumé you have so carefully prepared pays off. Your competition will probably forget to mention many of the seemingly mundane DP experience details that can propel them through stage 1 with flying colors. Your attention to detail in stage 1 points you out as a true DP professional. Any failure at detail singles you out as just another hacker.

A personal interview may be preceded by a phone screen. (A good agent will have prepared you for the call.) The rules of the personal interview apply here too. The phone screen can save you and the interviewer a lot of time, and you are not evaluated on the basis of your appearance. Your voice is very important. The phone screen gives you the interviewer's undivided attention and the opportunity to ask some significant questions that might not be answered from behind the interviewer's desk. If you pass the phone screen you will get a face-to-face interview and you will have gained three points.

The interview normally begins with a complete analysis of your background and the items on your detail résumé. You may be working with your interview résumé but presenting your credentials from your detail résumé. A sample of your work is always appropriate to establish credibility. If the interviewer is not interested, show him anyway; it's part of the sale. He will respect your aggressiveness. Stage 1 of the interview is your opportunity to present your accomplishments in the best possible light.

The interviewer will be looking for some of the following:

Depth and length of experience
Job continuity
Growth in responsibility
Salary progression
Your intelligence, competence, and strengths and weaknesses
Your verbal organization and ability to communicate
Your motivation, pride, ego, and enthusiasm
Your promotional potential

You must prove that you are the best of the competition, through organization, expression, communication, and competence. You are selling your total self. Recall, speed, and depth detail are attributes of a qualified DP professional.

Stage 1 only counts for 10 yards on the field toward the goal line. Some programmers actually believe they get hired because they can program. The DP ego is deceptive, probably because a junior person does learn a skill that others look up to, and it is easy to believe you are the greatest—but only as far as you can see. The interviews are your real competition.

I have known many job candidates who came out of interviews actually believing they had the job locked. Indeed they got all 10 points in stage 1, but failed to move down field after that. They didn't know how they appeared to others. Don't fall into the technical jargon trap if you are being interviewed by a nontechnical person.

The second stage of the interview will consist of questions to expose your personal characteristics, such as

1   What are your career objectives and goals?
    Goals count if they relate to the job at hand.

2   What are your strengths and weaknesses?
    Don't ever discuss your weaknesses, everybody has them. Substitute a strength, such as "work too hard to meet deadlines."

3   What type of position are you really seeking?
    It had better be the one you are interviewing for.

4   What has been your most significant accomplishments?
    It had better be job-related.

5   What salary are you looking for?
    Avoid a specific answer. "Depends on the opportunity" is one answer. "A reasonable offer" is another.

6   Why are you considering changing jobs?
    "Opportunity," of course, is the answer, or career improvement or more responsibility. Never money alone.

7   Tell me about yourself.
    Tell them about a job you have completed, not about yourself. Avoid complaints. No one really wants to hear them. Your personal life story is not important to any company.

8   What outside activities do you do?
    One non-job-related activity is enough. Professional job-related activities are the best.

9   What do you know about our company?
    You had better know something and express interest.

10 What other options are you exploring?
    Always have a couple; it shows you are actively looking.

11 What can you do for our company?
    Say what you have done for other companies and what you believe you can do at the next job level.

12 What will your references from your present and previous jobs say about you?
    Always pick the best and be specific concerning your accomplishments.

13 Could you stay with your present job?
Of course you can, but the pyramid is narrow and it could be a long wait.

14 How soon could you join us?
Two weeks to wind things down is always adequate.

15 How soon do you think it would be before you could be productive?
Three to six weeks shows the degree of confidence you have in your ability to learn.

16 Will you relocate for our company?
Absolutely. You can negotiate this after you are employed.

17 Why aren't you further along in your career age/job level?
A really tricky one: the answer is that you are more thorough than fast and spend a lot of time turning out quality work.

18 Have you ever hired or fired anyone? Why?
Never give a personal reason, only productivity in the interest of the company and the employee.

19 Whom do you admire most?
Your parents, of course: they were real workers and good people.

20 Are you a problem solver?
Give an example of a complex problem you have solved.

These pat questions and answers may seem foolish, but some company staff love them. So now you know what's expected if they start.

Listen carefully, and don't hedge. If there are any questions you don't like, just say, "Let me get back to you on that one." This gives you a good excuse for calling back, if you are interested in the job.

From the above questions and answers, you can see that you had better have your act together in stage 2. You must know yourself. The interviewer will want to see how you handle yourself. Some good DP interviewers will bounce you in a technical area of expertise, sometimes generating stress and pressure to see if you really know your subject. One bluff and you might as well wrap it up. If you don't know the answer, say so and ask for the answer.

There are so many questions an interviewer can ask that trying to have a quick standard answer for each is a waste of time, and you probably couldn't pull it off anyway. Therefore, you should simply have general answers that reflect who and what you are, depending on the general class of question. Your words, mannerisms, and dress will give the real answer, regardless of most contrived answers to questions. And they will like you because of or in spite of your answers. Artificials are always less than the real thing. Consider the basics needed for stage 2:

Honesty This is the most important characteristic. If you have trouble with the truth, out of fear or the urge to win, you lose. But you don't have to tell everything or take it too far.

Motivation   If you are not 100 percent attentive to the job at hand, interested in doing the job, and trying to discover what is going on, you lose. This includes a certain modicum of aggressiveness. Some companies want tigers and workaholics—other companies only want you to appear to be a tiger and then only on one side. Show interest and enthusiasm.

Clear headedness   If you know what is going on, can organize your thoughts, communicate, and structure what is being said and can state clearly what your attitude is, then you win. Total awareness is difficult to attain. Try to be perceptive.

Respect   If you can respect the interviewer and have sincere sympathy for his or her problems you will get respect. If you project a feeling of superiority or have to prove your superiority to the interviewer in any way, you lose respect. Super competence is more objectionable than incompetence, because you will disrupt the honored company pyramid. The pyramid must be preserved if you want the job.

Silence   If you know when to shut up and listen, you are rare. Most people want to talk and make their point too often. Silence can work for you. Enjoy it. Compel the interviewer to speak. Don't be compulsive or impulsive.

Moderation   If you have not deviated too far in your position on any subject, you win. Get radical in religion, politics, or the way a job has to be done, and you lose. Strike for the middle ground as in chess. Get locked in a corner and it's checkmate. A little humor will help preserve the moderate tone.

Composure   You have a tendency to be disorganized when your interviewers ask random questions. Always run in second gear to keep good control of yourself. If you are subject to two-on-one interviews, you can use the other two to keep each other busy while you buy time to respond. You must exude confidence in your ability to learn and do the job, or your interviewer will not have the same confidence in you.

Dress   The "dress for success" principle has been proved over and over again. You must look clean and well groomed and be dressed appropriately. You are your own walking advertisement. You are what the interviewer will be looking at. There are extremes both ways. A beginning programmer trainee wearing a $500 suit, a diamond stickpin, and a 2-carat ring can be as deviant as the DP manager candidate in a sweater, cowboy boots, and skull cap. Deviants in dress and most other things always lose.

Organization   Some questions will require you to organize what you have done. You have to be able to tell a story in specific terms that the interviewer can understand. You must know your facts, dates, and technical nomenclature. If you forget or are vague, your image is worsened. You must know your goal, make sure it is understood, and show how it qualifies you for the job at hand. Abraham Lincoln said, "Storytellers win a lot." From all of these basics the company interviewers will conclude whether you are competent, intelligent, realistic, trainable, likable, and whether you fit into their group. Conversely, you will determine the same about them. Your image will be established.

The paradox really is: if you win, you lose. The best you can hope for is a tie game where both sides score and benefit from the experience. You end up liking each other. An ounce of image is worth 100 pounds of program compilations.

If you do well in stage 2 you have gained another 60 yards on the field toward the goal line. Run through the question list in the summary and see whether you would pass.

In stage 2, the personnel representative can blackball you but cannot hire you. His interrogation will be more psychological than technical. For higher positions, a session with a psychologist is not rare. If such a session is required, you may be put through a battery of tests and interviews that are designed to examine your compatibility with existing management and to reveal any weaknesses in your character. If you are asked to look at pictures and write a story, three sentences are adequate. If you get emotional, you are insecure. If you are asked to look at inkblots and see things, be sure you invent a couple of things even if you see nothing—it's supposed to indicate creativity.

You can never go wrong by relating strongly to your family and friends. Once in a while, a company may request that you submit to a polygraph (lie detector) test if you are to be in a security position or around large sums of money. If you are honest you have nothing to worry about.

Stage 2 will probe what you must know about yourself. Evaluate yourself before the interview and then after the interview from the employer's point of view. There are no perfect people.

Are you

An extrovert or an introvert?

Forceful or weak?

Artistic or rough?

Team-oriented or an individual contributor?

Narrow/specialized or wide/diversified?

Emotionally mature?

A good communicator or a hesitator?

Analytical or generalized?

Self-confident or unsure?

Planning-or doing-oriented?

Emotionally well adjusted?

An initiator?

A good self-evaluator?

A job hopper?

Perceptive?

After you have had an opportunity to reveal your personal thoughts, feelings, character, and other personal attributes, the interviewer may begin telling you about the company. By now you could be on the 30-yard line. If your interview has been a screen only or if you have not gained enough ground, you will sense this. You may decide you have had enough and end the interview, or they may end it.

Terminate an unproductive interview quickly.

If you and the interviewer are still feeling comfortable, stage 3 can begin, or a second interview may be scheduled. Your questions will continue to reveal your intelligence, competence, and personality. The answers to the questions can reveal to you the character of the company and the interviewer.

Consider the difference between questions in the following groups. Don't ask questions whose answers you really should know as a result of your research.

What is the company product (You should know it!)
What future products is the company planning?

What are the sales and earnings of the company expected to be?
What are future objectives and goals of the company?
Why will the company be successful? What risks are there?

How does data processing support the company business?
How should data processing support future company business?
How is DP organized? What are the staff size, job classes, levels?
Will DP be reorganized in the future? Why? Why not?

What have been the successful DP projects in the past two years?
What new projects are planned and why?

Who are the data processing managers? What are their tenures, their backgrounds, their futures?

What has the DP staff turnover been and why?
What training, experience building, or tuition refund programs exist or are planned?

What have been the data processing staff movements, transfers or promotions in the past two years?
What is the boss really like? What makes him tick?
How does senior management back DP?
How do senior management and DP interact?
What specific job will I be expected to do? What is the next job it will qualify me for?

As these questions are answered, integrate the information with your own knowledge in appropriate areas. If you do not participate in this stage of the interview with good questions, you lose.

Clearly you will want to know what business applications system activities, technical activities, and computer hardware and software exist and are planned. The latest hardware and software do not always correspond with the best companies, but the on-order hardware/software status will indicate who is planning and who is not.

In your questioning you will want to look for the same characteristics as those that were expected of you:

Honesty	Respect	Composure
Motivation	Silence	Dress
Clarity	Moderation	Organization

The most important aspect in stage 3 (your questions) is not to react to your discoveries. Most DP professionals lose yardage at this point. If you are not 100 percent positive in your stage 3 reaction, you lose. Most DP professionals forget that they are after an offer of employment and are not on a consulting engagement. They frequently show concern over this or that aspect of the job, which makes the interviewer become concerned as to whether they would work out in the situation.

One candidate showed concern over the percent of travel. The company wanted 50 percent, he wanted 20 percent. The impassee came on this point. It was a good match and a career opportunity. The candidate was unable to understand the art of gentle negotiation. If he had simply set aside the concern over travel and obtained the offer, the commitment would have been made. Then, he could have negotiated the level of travel down. The sequence is to first get an offer, then work on areas of concern and negotiate to what you want, not vice versa.

Another candidate voiced concern over the type of computer hardware on order. Instead of voicing support to get on with what seemed otherwise a good company and situation, he nitpicked it to death. He could have gotten the offer as manager of computer planning and made his recommendation for new hardware after he was in the position of holding an offer or being in the position. Most things are negotiable, but few DP-ers have a good sense of timing. He lost in stage 3.

Stage 3 is a time to ask questions and listen, not to voice concerns or criticize previous company decisions. They are going to hire you because you express certainty, not skepticism. Listen and evaluate what the total situation is so that the entire offer can be evaluated subsequently. If you start evaluation and response in stage 3, you lose. Of course, you must get all the facts so that if you have an offer, you can determine what you can negotiate or change later, but not in stage 3. Timing is everything; you must have time to compare your offers. If they don't make you an offer, there is nothing to be concerned about anyway.

Many DP candidates cannot see that many of their concerns are superficial from the viewpoint of the company. If you want many offers to choose from, concentrate on what's in it for the company in hiring you. Your offer hinges on how the company values your potential contribution. Your acceptance hinges on how you value the company contribution to your career. Get the offer first. Remember: The only perfect situations are in the minds of perfectionists.

Always get a tour of the DP facilities. You will be able to tell a lot from the computer room and programming facilities. Then get out fast. Too much time can result in overexposure. Always get back to your agent. He can frequently get a reading on your performance within hours after your interview.

If you passed the interview, stage 4 begins. You should have some indication from the interviewer. A second interview may be set up to have others confirm your technical and personal qualifications. You may be asked to comment on a general salary range. You may wish to indicate that the range is good or a little lower than you expected, but that you would consider all aspects of the job. If they like you, let the company reach a little. They must make the first move.

If the company asks for references, you are probably a candidate for an offer. A typical holding strategy of a company is to tell you they are interviewing several candidates and will get back to you. You may want to pin a company first on these points at the start of your interview. Some companies want to interview twenty candidates over a month and then give you one day to respond to their offer. Always indicate you have other interviews, and will probably be moving in a week or so. It will speed things up a bit.

The fact that you may be able to get an offer from a company should not be so gratifying that you automatically take it—at least not the first offer. The company is evaluating you along with several other candidates. You must also evaluate the company, experience to be gained, the career move, the new boss, a lateral versus vertical move, and lastly what two to three years on the new job will add to your detail résumé in terms of your DP career plan and overall worth.

You will note that so far, little or no mention has been made of salary. For negotiation purposes, the most important interview factor is mutual need, not how much salary you will have to have. The salary currently earned is frequently only a starting base. If you are far under or over what your competition is ready to quote, you have a special problem. Of course, company budgets for specific positions have ranges, but both candidates and companies have reasons to negotiate when a mutual interest is solid.

You can fail stage 4 if you are impatient, immature, and do not understand the art of gentle pursuasion. Most DP candidates don't.

If you are interviewed by a structured company and by more than two people, more than likely they will complete an interview form on you. The rating questions are frequently as follows (rated from 1 to 5).

Appearance	Experience
Friendliness	Drive
Poise and stability	Overall ability
Personality	Hire, yes or no
Conversationability	Future hire, yes or no
Alertness	Best qualified for what type of work
General knowledge of job	Comments

Evaluate yourself on the basis of these factors for each interview.

REFERENCES

One of the most important factors in stage 4 concerns who will "testify." Your best reference is a former boss who liked you and appreciated your work. You must choose your references carefully and always let them know that a check is imminent. Know where they are. Have phone numbers of home and work. Let them know the typical types of questions which can be asked. Long detailed responses are not required. Make sure they keep it short and sweet.

The following are some typical questions put to references:

1   Do you know Mark French?
2   What were his dates of employment?
3   What position did he hold? What was his salary?
4   What was the quality and quantity of his work?
5   What was your relative position to him in the company; management, peer, subordinate?
6   What were his reviews like?
7   Would you rehire him? Why? Why not?
8   Do you know anyone else who is familiar with his work?
    (A real tricky one— now you have lost control.) Alert your references to have them ask you directly.
9   What are his strengths?
10 What are his weaknesses? *(Have them substitute a strength.)*
11 Do you think he is management material? Why?
12 Could he manage a group of ten specialists? If not, why not?
13 Is he a tiger or a wimp, firm or soft?

If your references are quite positive, they can frequently set you up for a better offer than you expect. Of course, references from management are more important than from peers, peers are more important than subordinates, and subordinates are more important than others outside the company, unless they are fairly high up in an organization.

Frequently, in the interview, the conversation reaches a point where you innocently talk of various people, vendors, or audit firms with which you are acquainted. Be very careful in discussing these situations because they may be the first to be contacted for references without your knowledge. Again, you can lose control. Since these same vendors or audit firms may have a direct line to your company, you may be compromised. Most vendor and auditor firms will protect their client first and handle the ethics afterwards. Alas, it's a cruel world—life in the big city!

THE CHECKLIST

Organize for selling and communicating. Be organized. Use your detail résumé.

1   Be on time for the interview—it reflects favorably on you. Be rested.

2   Dress well. Look sharp but conservative—proper dress is associated with good work.

3   Bring your interview résumé—it's the format of the interview.

4   Know whether you will relocate, and know where the job is.

5   Know whether you will travel and what percentage of time.

6   Know whether you will work long hours—overtime, Saturdays, second and third shifts.

7   Shake hands firmly—don't be a wimp.

8   Speak clearly, crisply—communicate. Don't use slang. Avoid "yup/nope," "you know." Don't ramble; make your point concisely.

9   Listen 60 percent of the time. Never cut off the interviewer or interrupt. No speeches.

10   Maintain eye contact. Keep your eyes on the interviewer's—the eyes will tell you everything.

11   Be serious, be cheerful, smile. No wisecracks, no lies.

12   Don't complain about anything—present boss, company, salary, and so forth.

13   Indicate your interest in the job and your profession.

14   Be impressed by the efforts and the work of the company. Avoid telling them what they should have done. You may ask whether they have considered this or that approach.

15   Don't smoke, chew, eat, or drink during the interview.

16   Have your job references ready and be sure to check them out first. One poor reference can squelch an offer.

17   Thank the interviewer. It takes so little effort on your part.

18   Don't exaggerate anything or brag. Don't display egos.

19   Don't comment on superfluous subjects, for example, office, building, people.

20   Ask for the job if you want it: "I hope you consider me."

21   Remain calm, don't fidget.

22   Don't say sir or madam. No parent-child relationships are allowed.

23   Remember names and use them.

24   Demonstrate interest—stay awake!

25 Know your detail résumé by heart.

26 Know yourself—objectives, goals, career strengths.

27 Know your weaknesses and have answers down pat:

Why are you leaving your current position?

Why were you fired?

Why did you change jobs?

Why did you have a low grade-point average?

Why are you an alcoholic?

Why were you divorced?

Why is there an employment gap?

Why is your progress slow for your age or experience?

What is your arrest record?

Why do you have no degree?

28 Ask good questions, for example on the following subjects:

Company product

Company financial data

Company stock and ownership

Company growth record

Company plants and size

Company competition

Company customers

The DP plans and budget

The DP hardware and software

Here are the accounts of a few real-life cases. See if you could have given these DP-ers any advice.

The Case of Steve

Steve was a programmer skilled in RPG II programming. Steve had an associate degree in computer science and three years of solid experience and knew his hardware and software and business applications well. Steve's résumé showed two employers in the last three years. At an interview with a smaller company, Steve successfully passed interview stages 1, 2, and 3. During the interview Steve chatted informally with the company controller, who learned that the company's auditors were the auditors for Steve's current employer. Steve was asked to leave a couple of references. Within a couple of hours, the company controller called the audit firm and inquired about Steve. The audit firm promised to check it out and call the controller back. The audit firm promptly called their other client to notify them that one of their programmers was looking.

When Steve returned, his boss told him if he interviewed anywhere again he would be immediately terminated. The audit firm told the prospective new employer that Steve's present company was not too pleased with him and that he was only a marginal worker. Steve did not get an offer.

References?

The Case of John

John had three years of college and an extensive 20-year career in DP ranging from programmer to senior systems analyst, with 3- to 5-year tenure in seven companies. John was looking to move up but could not seem to make it in his present company, a profitable manufacturer. Earning $23K, John began interviewing but with little success. He finally got an interview with a company for a project manager position. John successfully passed interview stages 1, 2, and 3. The company indicated that they might be able to offer $26K. John hesitated for the following reasons:

1 The company wanted him to program 20 percent. He felt he was above all of that.
2 The company was a little too far for him to drive (30 minutes). He would not move.
3 Possibly things were not too bad where he was—he was coming up for a raise in five months.
4 He thought he should have an offer of at least $30K to move.
5 He declined the offer.

One month after his offer refusal, his company terminated a few people, including him. John had to take what he could get at a hospital—full-time programming job at $21.5K, with an hour's drive to work. Is John a planner, realistic, on the move, introspective or a decision maker?

Moving up?

The Case of Bob

Bob had a BS and an MS in mathematics with high honors from a good midwestern school. He had a scientific programming job with a medium-size engineering and consulting firm. After four years, a management change reduced his responsibilities from those of a project group leader to those of a senior programmer. Most of his work has been in FORTRAN, and he also had a little COBOL, but little in the way of business application programming.

After four interviews he had still failed to get an offer, even though he had indicated he would accept a lateral for $21.5K. Bob checked his references and could find no poor reports. Two companies told him they found other candidates which fit their requirements better. Bob then invested a year in evening COBOL courses and basic business studies. After two more interviews with premier companies, Bob still did not get an offer. A friend at one of the companies he interviewed told him that he had heard they didn't think he was too friendly. Bob decided to try for an MBA and went back to school again. Did Bob know what his problem was?

Chemistry?

The Case of Nathan

Nathan had a business degree and five years of COBOL programming on minor vendor hardware in a manufacturing environment. Nathan believed other new members of the staff were approaching his salary level and that he should have a raise. After a few delays, Nathan decided to see what he could get on the open market. After a successful interview he received an offer of $1.5K more than he was earning. He presented the offer to his DP manager, who immediately presented an argument to the finance VP. Both Nathan, and the DP manager expected some kind of salary adjustment for Nathan. The VP for finance called his favorite personnel agency and gave them specifications on the jobs for DP manager and programmer. In three weeks the new staff arrived; both employees were demoted to programmer positions and subsequently left the company.

End run?

The Case of Mike

Mike had started his DP career as a computer operator and in eighteen years had progressed to DP manager with a medium-size retailer. He had continued his education and had one year to go for his BS degree. A friend told him of an opening as an operations planner at a major bank for $3K more than he was making. Mike interviewed and accepted the position, but after one year discovered that the pace and type of work were not what he enjoyed. He stuck it out for another six months and finally decided to leave. He terminated his employment to search for a job full time and to take a vacation.

To Mike's surprise, he could not find many interviews and received no offers. The economy turned down and his savings were declining faster than he had planned. Mike was able to find a few temporary jobs as a programmer, but for less than he had made five years ago.

In each subsequent job interview, the companies asked why he had not progressed further. The bank refused to rehire him, but gave him a good reference. Mike finally got rehired at his previous retail employer, but as an assistant store manager at a little less than he made as DP manager. What advice can you give Mike?

Planning?

The Case of Larry

Larry had a BS and an MS in economics with a minor in accounting. He had held increasingly good jobs over a ten-year period, ranging from programmer to senior systems analyst. Larry interviewed for a technical support manager job and successfully passed stages 1, 2, and 3 with a DP manager and the controller of the firm. After receiving an offer of $3K more than he was making, Larry made a list of all of the DP department deficiencies he had observed during a one-day preliminary study of his potential new company. Larry decided to decline the offer but spent two hours with the controller presenting his findings and solutions.

The controller subsequently offered Larry a newly created position as MIS director. There was good chemistry. Larry accepted, provided he would have full responsibility and authority to significantly improve the DP department. He got it.

Maneuver?

The Case of Tom

Tom was a fast-track senior programmer with a degree in business administration earning $23K with a manufacturing company. After three years spent implementing some major projects, Tom interviewed with a competing firm for a project leader position. This firm was about to embark on a system expansion similar to what Tom had helped to implement at his current company. During the interview Tom volunteered to the DP manager the information that the plans for the new manufacturing system were not in the correct sequence and in fact the wrong hardware and software were selected and on order. It was clear that Tom had precisely the kind of talent the company needed. Other members of the company management were highly enthusiastic about Tom's ability, communication style, and knowledge. The DP manager wanted to interview as many candidates as possible to find the best one. After thirty days of interviewing, the DP manager had to go to a seminar and volunteered that he thought Tom was a little overpriced. Luckily, Tom was able to find another position before the DP manager had to make a decision. The company found someone who fit in better with the staff.

Threat?

The Case of Jim

Jim had a degree in mathematics, with in-depth technical support background in communications and data base software internals. He had held three jobs over an eleven-year period. He was mainly looking for a technical challenge. Jim listed with an agent who widely circulated his résumé showing current earnings of $26K. A company bidding on a government contract immediately made a contingency offer of $32.5K by mail without any other contact with Jim, asking to use his résumé in bidding for the contract. No interview was required.

Research?

SUMMARY

The prime reason you pass an inteview is because they like you. A personable approach is key. If you like them, chances are they will like you. If you don't qualify for one job, there may be another they will consider you for.

Remember, *interview, interview, interview.*

The more skill you develop in this activity, the faster you will know yourself and can propel yourself up the EDP pyramid. It costs you nothing but a little time.

If you don't get an offer, you must know why, so that you don't continue to make the same errors. Again, good references can make the difference.

The purpose of this chapter is to help you understand the interview and its subtleties. By knowing basically what to expect you are in a better position to evaluate the company and maximize your offer potential.

If you have been successful in finding the next career step position and getting an offer, you can then accept, reject, or negotiate. A large percentage of DP candidates are totally blind to negotiation possibilities. How many times I have heard the DP candidate say, "They just didn't offer enough money," without giving any thought to benefits, long-term career growth, or a six-month subsequent pay adjustment.

If you get an offer, you have scored.

Seven

Get the Maximum Offer

TIMING IS CRITICAL

The job offer is a distinct and separate activity after the interview. Often an applicant and a potential employer discuss salaries before the job is even addressed. You may not be aware of the actual level of the job for which you can qualify within the new company. This mistake is probably a result of neither party understanding the hiring process or the advantage of separating these two activities. An applicant may blow his best career opportunity simply by immediately overpricing or underpricing himself.

Applicants frequently do not know how to determine or sell their worth to a particular company, and companies often embarrass themselves by quoting a salary level before the applicant understands the full career possibilities. It is okay simply to suggest that you will discuss salary only after your background and the company opportunities are fully explored.

After you and the employer fully agree that the available job is a desirable opportunity and that you have the qualifications, salary can always be negotiated.

From an applicant's point of view, there are offers and then there is the *best* offer. Often the applicant has no idea of evaluation criteria for one offer over another other than salary. Companies often do not understand how to present their opportunity so as to beat their competition and hire the best applicant.

If an applicant is underpaid in his current position, a substantial increase may still only bring him to less then the bottom of the salary range that the hiring company intended to offer.

A job offer may take several weeks after the interview to materialize. Sometimes the offer will come only after a second interview, or it may come on the spot. Several candidates may be considered and many reference checks may be necessary to confirm employment earnings, experience, and personal characteristics. Some companies are open to negotiation. Others make a set offer, and that's it.

Some insist on written offers, while others will extend a verbal offer to test the applicant's sincerity. Some companies start with a low offer and then inch their way up. Some companies will allow your agent to submit the tentative offer to you before the formal offer, to eliminate the delays of counteroffers. These companies like to give offers which are acceptable the first time and know you will accept. In these cases, your agent is in an excellent position to negotiate for you and avoid any sudden turnoffs.

Always know what your minimum acceptable salary will be, so that no matter how sudden or what form the offer takes, you can "tentatively" accept on the spot. You may not get a second chance. It is always easier to continue negotiations after an acceptance than after an initial rejection. Acceptance can tie you in and keep the company door open while negotiations continue. You will be surprised how easily you can train a company to negotiate with you. There is no rule that can't be changed or an offer that can't be expanded. All things are possible.

OFFER CONTENTS AND EVALUATION

Several factors enter into your evaluation of an offer. Obviously, you want to select a profitable and well-run company that supports the DP activity and understands the need for good DP techniques.

The job must fit your long-range career plan. You cannot waste time on a sidetrack, regardless of salary, because you may not be able to get back into the mainstream. If you are deficient in technology you may trade salary for a learning opportunity. You must not slip into a highly paid specialty that narrows the chances for long-term progress. Know what jobs you will be working on.

Make sure you know the next step up in the company and how long it may take you to achieve it. If this vital information is missing, reject the offer.

Know how long your prospective boss has been in his position. If he has just arrived, you could move with him. If he has been in his position for a substantial length of time, chances are that you will have to move around him, or you may soon have a new boss. If that happens, the new boss will have to use up your career time to evaluate you for promotion. Know the boss's age and evaluate his job and experience. Will he teach you or will you be used to teach him. Has he been passed over for higher jobs? Has another boss been promoted over him as the company grew?

Know the reputation of the DP shop. What has happened to others? Is there a high turnover? Are there good salary advances and educational and training opportunities? You must check company references also. Don't be afraid to ask for some. The company is not afraid to ask yours.

If the position is a new one, evaluate the degree to which management supports its responsibilities. If the position is established, you will evaluate why the vacancy exists, how it was performed, where the previous holder went, and why. You must explore the job responsibilities, performance standards, objectives, and goals of the position. Typically, these standards will include the following:

Planning systems development

Systems design

Program specifications

Programming

Communication with management, peers, subordinates, and system users

Personal development

Supervisory and management skills

The companies' expectations may exceed your capability to get the job done, it may be impossible even for a magician to meet the projected schedules or to get a good review. Don't settle for a challenge with a loaded deck.

Find out what authority you will have to get the job done. Your ability to hire, terminate, or budget is crucial to success. Some authority, however, belongs to those who assume it.

Finally, can you realistically climb the DP and company pyramid, or is the opportunity just a myth?

Company politics can play a significant role. Try to find out whether there is a lot of enthusiasm, esprit de corps, favoritism, nepotism, optimism, or pessimism. You can usually tell whether or not those with whom you have interviewed believe in the company and the general situation.

Offers usually contain some of the components listed below. Your evaluation depends on the weight you assign to each component.

Ongoing Job Factors	**Consideration**
Salary	Is it a good increase over what you earn?
Cost of living	These adjustments can be substantial.
Job level	Is it a move up in responsibility, title?
Job class	Will it broaden your experience?
Education/training	Will it teach you a great deal? Is there tuition reimbursement?
Career	Does it support your long-term career plans? Are there assignment guarantees?

Performance review	Does it offer regular performance reviews?
Benefit	Are there substantial medical, life, disability, dental, and optical insurance benefits?
Equity	Do stock options, profit-sharing, saving, or stock-purchase plans exist?
Retirement	Do substantial pension or retirement plans exist? Who contributes, and how much? When are you vested?
Bonus	Is there any opportunity to earn a bonus on the basis of your performance or of company performance? Is it guaranteed or discretionary?
Vacations/time off	Is the job an 80-hour per week standard?
Holidays	Can you accrue vacation time or compensatory time off for overtime?
Overtime	Whether you are paid by the hour or by salary, you should know if you are expected to work 40 or 80 hours per week and if you get overtime pay.
Free parking	It can save you a significant amount.
Company car	This represents a significant supplement to your salary.
Expense account	Should depend on type of position.
Company cafeteria	Lunches add up quickly.
Distance to work	Consider the price of gasoline, travel, and fatigue.
Industry	Is it one you can be interested in?
Company	Is it growing, profitable, DP-oriented?
Computer hardware/software	Will knowledge of it further your long-range career?
Job location	Do you want to make a career in Alaska?
Memberships	To expand your ongoing professional status
The area	Think of the cost of housing, food, real estate, mortgage rates, clothing, recreation, fuel, and so forth.

One-Time Job Factors	Consideration
Advance start date	Would be important in the event of immediate termination by your current company.
Salary review	A six-month salary review guarantee could add to your initial earnings base.
Housing	Is there one-time housing bonus or new mortgage opportunity?
Interim living	Is there a 30- to 60-day interim living reimbursement for a new location?
House hunt	A fully paid trip to the location to search for a new home would help.
Home mortgage acquisitions	Ask about mortgage assumptions, interest differentials, home purchases.
Payroll dating	Ask to be placed on the payroll with subsequent time off to move.
Termination agreement	Try to get a one-year termination pay, if for any reason the company eliminates your position within one year, plus a continuation on benefits for six months.
Moving expenses	Get an all-expenses-paid move of household goods and possessions, including utility hookups.
Agency fees	The company should pay all agency fees. You should be liable for no fees even if you quit. Sign nothing, it's to your disadvantage.

Always get all of the information relevant to the ongoing and one-time factors of the offer before accepting.

OFFER NEGOTIATIONS

You or your agent can negotiate any remuneration factors of the job. It is always appropriate to ask that all the job offer factors to be put in writing to avoid any future misunderstandings. Using your agent to negotiate these factors keeps you out of any confrontation with the company and avoids preemployment embarrassments.

If you have two or more job offers, you or your agent can communicate certain aspects of other offers to the company you want to work for and often can obtain some of the good features of other offers. You can obtain the best of all worlds.

Some companies may want you to sign a one-year nontermination agreement, obligating you to remain for one year, expecially if they are incurring a major expense in hiring you. Sign it; it's not enforceable and companies feel more secure. If you want to leave, you simply violate a company rule such as not showing up for work because you are on an interview. If they want to play, you play too. Remember, though, don't sign any agency fee repayment agreements. Before you accept, update your résumé and see how the potential job adds to your career.

GIVING NOTICE TO YOUR EMPLOYER

When you have accepted an offer from another company, it is important to establish a firm starting date. You must be prepared, at worst, to accept an immediate termination from your present employer. Most companies regard two weeks as acceptable notice. Data processing professionals are usually very dedicated and sometimes feel obligated to stay on three to four weeks to wind things down and train a replacement. This is usually because companies do not adequately staff backups, provide training for backup, and often stretch data processors across many applications. A company can sometimes actually make you feel guilty for leaving. After all, they trained you. Then why didn't they pay you at going rates and give you enough so that a job change would be out of the question? Forget about counteroffers. If the company didn't appreciate your work until you gave notice or got another offer, why should you believe your disloyalty will change their practices? For company convenience, they may boost your salary until they find someone else to protect their interests. But after giving notice, you will always be suspect. Relationships will never be the same.

Most companies feel that once you have decided to leave, having you around would only create discontent in others. Therefore it is in the best interest of the company to terminate you immediately or as soon as possible. If you have vacation pay due, try to get it in advance payments before you give notice. Some employees have been bewildered by companies that immediately terminated them and all their benefits, including accrued vacation upon receiving notice from the employee. Clearly in your own best interest and for the sake of future references (which you will ultimately need), be careful not to downgrade your present company or any individual. You may feel a certain hostility, but any expression of discontent can hurt only you, not the company. Don't flatter yourself that your parting advice, as a lame duck, will make any difference whatsoever. Conversely, if you leave your company with good wishes from and to the entire staff, you have contributed significantly to your stature as an individual and to your career. Let it be known that you are leaving only because of an opportunity to gain wider experience and to move upward. Who can argue with that?

If you can get a written reference from your boss or other management personnel it can be important to you in the future. Also, it is important that your termination record indicate that you are eligible for rehire. People at the company may move on, but the termination record remains for future reference checks.

Leaving your friends, work, and familiar surroundings can be an unsettling experience. However, you, your family, your earnings, and career cannot wait. Your productive years and opportunities are finite.

THE NEW JOB

So there you are. The going-away parties are over and you have successfully arrived at the new company. You have made it, right? Wrong! More careers are finished at the new company the first day at work than can be counted.

From the first day, you must ensure that the job and circumstances are as represented. If there are any variations in your understanding of the job (title, pay, expenses, etc.), get them clarified as soon as possible. You have the most leverage on the first day. Then after that it's a down-hill ride to achieve a high degree of credibility and a base of management support. Start from the first day to complete all assignments as if they were the most important in the company. Respect begets respect. Display the traits that got you the job and proceed as if you planned to be with the new company for the rest of your working years.

Don't lose contact with your agent or companies that have made you offers. If you find that you have made a mistake in taking any job, the quicker you get going again the better. You can't be faulted for making a mistake, but leaving after six months will have to be explained throughout your career and will cause suspicions of unreliability in other potential employers. Murphy's Law: If something can go wrong, it will.

SUMMARY

The purpose of this chapter is to help you evaluate job offers and to negotiate successfully that which is negotiable. The main focus is on evaluating new company jobs, but the criteria can also be used to compare succeeding jobs within your own company. Your success within your own company depends on your ability to ensure that you receive full credit and recognition for your performance.

You must be sure you have agreements with your management on what the job is, the standards of performance, and the criteria for evaluation and review. Each performance and salary review can be compared with the interview and offer for a new job.

Whether you accept the new offer, continue your current job search, or elect to stay put in the same company, you have made a decision. The cycle continues whether you advance within your current company or change companies periodically. Unfortunately, in our society a prejudice exists against those who stay with a company only a year or two and then move on. Somehow the company is seen to be something sacred instead of as a department of The American Industry. When other professionals change locations, take new contracts, or join other members of their profession in joint ventures, it is frequently viewed as a natural evolution. Keep in mind, however, that if total paternalism prevailed, no company would ever take from another without the latter's permission or terminate your employment to maintain the bottom line.

The major advantage of The American Free Enterprise System is the mobility of talented resources to relevant areas in the supply/demand arena. Talent can and does seek its own level, especially in DP activities. It is clear that there must be a good proportion of Chiefs to Indians, even in data processing.

Above all, you must know whether you can and want to achieve higher levels of DP competence. Not everyone is destined to be a pyramid head. Some DP professionals have advanced from one level to another until they have reached incompetence in the job they hold. Some DP managers should have had the sense not to take the final offer: they might have been happier in their last area of high competence, even at a slightly lower rate of pay.

Eight

Stay at the Top
of the Pyramid

VIEW FROM THE TOP

When you finally approach the top of the EDP pyramid you will have mixed feelings depending on how you got there and the security you feel inside. You may be one of the choosen few, but the question is, how long will you survive? Will you leap to the top of another pyramid, be replaced as the organization grows, fall quickly down the pyramid, hold your position, or advance to a non-EDP position in the company.

The paradox in the successful DP career is that frequently the DP professional loses touch with the very functions in which he or she was so proficient. Management, administration, planning, controlling, budgeting, and personnel are a long way from the COBOL coding pad. If you are with a small or unsophisticated company, they may also expect you to code and sweep up.

For the first time the buck stops with you. Responsibility for DP is no small assignment, for you are expected to communicate effectively with your peers (who are non-EDP-oriented), with a boss (who may know nothing of the technicalities and problems), and with an EDP staff (who are highly mobile, aggressive, and perhaps incompetent). Are you sure you really are ready for this job or even want it? You clearly want the money, control, power, and maybe the prestige: but the responsibility, headaches, long hours, personnel problems, and performance demands can ruin your health and split your family. Remember, he who would lead must be of service to all (author unknown).

By the time you have been hired for or promoted to the DP head position, you are aware of some of the pitfalls. The budget is never adequate to meet all of the demands or the required schedules for DP implementation. There are never enough talented people to staff your organization, even with an open budget. Few outside of DP understand why "these things" take so long and cost so much, fail so often, or in some cases are even needed at all. Documentation is never complete, and often the wheel must be invented over and over again. Some salesman, consultant, or staff member is always presenting some technology which is supposed to be a better mousetrap for a lower operating cost. What does it matter if the conversion ties up the whole DP staff for a year and completely disjoints an operating department for two years. The price of progress may be your job. You are the top man, but you are also the whipping boy for every one in the company, down to the mail girl who didn't get her check.

To make progress, you wear two hats. You are the coach for your staff, but you also have to put up with the owner of the team and face the wrath of the fans. Lose a few games and they get a new coach. There is no time to rest because the season never ends. Have you ever wondered where the old DP managers and directors end up? This job is impossible, if the company is growing at all. Because of all of this, your job hunting will continue even when you are at the top. If your boss doesn't get you, your peers, your staff, or you yourself may do you in, just when you think everything is going along okay. To survive you must continue to develop, but not necessarily along DP lines.

YOUR BOSS

The most important aspect of any DP management job is the boss. You must choose your boss carefully as your EDP head, because his background, aspirations, expectations, motivation, and temperament will make you or break you. Sometime during your career, the boss you have may be replaced by one not of your choosing. You may have progressed well with the old boss, but you can be sure that when the new boss arrives, it's a whole new ballgame.

If you have personality conflicts with the boss, they will block your path to success and surely eat away at your physical and mental health. A five-year DP manager with a medium-sized growing manufacturer found this out. The new controller arrived on the scene. The DP manager had built the DP department from scratch. He had written many of the operational programs when he was a programmer. He knew most of the plant managers, had a good knowledge of the business, and had been promoted twice to reach his present position. The new controller had been brought in to assist in an expansion of the business by the owner, who knew that operating on a larger basis required new kinds of people, people different from those who had been responsible for getting it to where it was (a not uncommon dilemma).

Totally unprepared, the DP manager could not stifle his ego. He had to display that he knew more than the controller about what was currently going on, despite the fact he did not have a degree. Instead of being smart about what had happened, he took up the impossible crusade to beat his boss. He overestimated his own value to the company and tried numerous end runs. The controller saw what was happening, promoted the systems supervisor to DP manager, and put the old DP manager on special projects, reporting to the controller. Then, after two months, the controller convinced the owner that there was really no place for the old DP manager to go within the company. The old DP manager was allowed to resign. If you can't be supportive of the boss, it's only a matter of time.

As you climb the EDP pyramid, your boss becomes increasingly important and you must see eye to eye as a team. In the beginning, they gave you a program to write and either it worked or it didn't. As you progress in DP activities, subjective judgment of you and the boss become the key to longevity.

You must analyze the boss's background, objectives, and goals. If he has come up through the ranks, the boss may have very little DP background. Frequently the boss of DP is a financial type who has counted the beans all of this life. He may have never have had to plant, harvest, or sell anything. To him, all EDP ventures may be strictly dollar-and-cent decisions. In fact, the accountant-type officer can be so conservative that you have to give him hours of computer philosophy instructions to make him realize why he should approve time-sharing terminals for programmers. You can get caught in his "paralysis" of "analysis."

The typical financial-type boss will push his financial report projects ahead of plant automation projects every time. He may in fact have his own little games going on with his peers.

Conversely, there are some outstanding accounting-type bosses who highly respect the problems of DP implementation. They are eager to give you the opportunity to show what you and your staff can do. If your boss takes you to meetings with his boss and gives you freedom to speak and supports you, he is one of the few. If you are isolated from your boss's boss, it's time to leave. Remember he has your future in his hand.

Of course, if you could pick a boss, it would be the chief executive officer (CEO) of the company. It is clear that the number one DP person in progressive companies always reports to the CEO because DP serves all company pyramid heads. The CEO has to be the tie breaker in questions of which department or division gets priority for advanced computerization for the overall good of the company. Electronic data processing activities are simply too expensive to plan, implement, and operate for money to be spent foolishly.

Regardless of which boss you finally end up with, the real clincher is you yourself. You may be a good technician, but now you must be a supurb people person or you lose. Sooner or later you are no longer dealing only with DP people, who understand what you are talking about when you use technical jargon. You now have to communicate in terms of business activities.

You must be able to see that the boss is human too. You have to be able to show him how you are helping him achieve his goals. One of the biggest causes of DP management failure is the inability of DP managers to communicate with management in non-DP terms. Use your standard buzz word generator a few times and you lose. When you can break down the issues and show cost/benefit relationships to your boss, he will understand what you are doing and defend you.

Frequently DP managers believe they are actually listening to their bosses and communicating. They think they are doing the job. Because the boss respects them for their EDP knowledge and motivation, he is reluctant to tell them that they just aren't listening. Discreetly he looks for your replacement. It is very easy to let the boss's words go in one ear and out the other, then to proceed the way you know it has to be done anyway. Some DP mustangs believe they wrote the book and are experts on most things. When egos clash, it is frequently the DP professional who loses and fails to see why he was not clever enough to control himself.

Dependency is a key factor to tune in to. If the boss needs you a great deal, you are secure, but he may elect to block your promotion and advancement. Dependency is the basis of your contract. A good boss will not block you or stand in your way. He will promote you to wherever he can. He will train you and protect you. If you do the same for him, you will build a better career. Boss chemistry is everything.

YOUR PEERS

As you approach the top of the EDP pyramid your peers will be more varied in their experience and interests. When you were a programmer, the programmers shared your DP addiction. As a DP management person, you will find fewer things to share with your peers unless you have greatly expanded your interests and learning base. Most DP managers fail to grow into top positions because they cannot keep up with their peers. A common myth is that DP has to be formally brought to the VP level. Frequently, it is only because the DP man has developed himself to assume the broad responsibilities of that level that a DP vice president exists. Most DP managers do not do this.

In the course of your career, your peers frequently determine where you will go. Your peer communication skills and support will affect their comments. Some DP management failures have waged running battles with their peers, to the point where the senior management have finally had enough and have gotten a new leader. Because you and your staff are often responsible for changing the way your peers and their staff operates, you are in a precarious position. If your system solution causes them to falter in their mission, you can be sure they will not go down alone. Conversely, if you really help them, word of mouth will keep your raises coming.

It is easy to criticize what is going on in the operations of your company's other divisions and to remark about how screwed up things are, but remember, everything that goes around comes around.

It will be easy to observe how your staff and your peer's staff actually cooperate to produce some fine systems when you and your divisional peer are frequently seen together in a good mood. Conversely, when you and your peers are engaged in memos wars (with copies to the world) you cannot win, even if you are right 70 percent of the time.

Peer chemistry is second only to boss chemistry in the world of DP implementation. As in interviewing for a job, servicing your peers consists of more than slide shows of DP technology and the wonderful computer world of the future. The real key is the personality of your peers: their characters, aspirations, motivations—what makes them tick.

Data processing management is a system of human relations: the elusive system of cooperative effort for the synergistic benefit. The "how" of the new computer data base has a much lower priority to your job success.

If there is harmony between you and your peers, all of your system mistakes (of which there will always be many) will be worked around and swept under the rug. If there is a clash between you and your peers, every error of addition will be exposed as if it had just destroyed the company's business.

Many DP executives hide within the walls of the computer mystique. You have to get out among your users and listen, listen, listen. They may look to you for direction, which is a great ego booster. Give them education instead, then let them tell you. If you play the role of the dictator, you ultimately will be shot. If you are a good teacher, you may get to teach next year. Your peers are an excellent source of training in their own specialties: accounting, finance, marketing, manufacturing, and others.

Your power comes in the pivotal position between peers. It is a delicate situation in which you can never take sides.

YOUR STAFFING

When you attain a DP management position, you will frequently be attracted to hiring people with personalities and dispositions like your own. In this regard, there probably couldn't be a worse choice.

What is important in staffing the DP department is intelligence, competence, honesty, motivation, and dedication. Remember what it was like when you were coming up the DP pyramid. Data processing people today cannot be misled into believing that they will be with the company forever, nor can you. All of you will be moving: some up, some over, and some down.

Managing the DP staff is much more complex than any other type of activity. Just as you had to learn the complexities of your non-EDP boss and peers, you now have to know the things that make a good DP staff go or stay.

Clearly, leading-edge hardware and software make a difference in attracting and holding good lower-level staff. Training schools and cross-fertilization among staff members is important and should be cultivated, but we all know how difficult that is because good tradesmen tend to keep their tricks to themselves.

The awarding of battle ribbons helps some, but not a lot. What is it then that produces a top-notch staff?

This author believes that it is freedom with responsibility. Tight control in DP produces a stale staff. It is impossible to grow without the freedom to make mistakes. Data processing staffs want good communication from the top, freedom to discuss alternative solutions, and the opportunity for discovery—the only way to learn. Of course, freedom can be carried to the point where you are getting only one line of code produced per day, or where system designs are repeated daily with no end in sight.

When your staff feels you are a dictator and your way always wins, you have failed as a DP manager. It is possible to know too much and insist on covering all of the bases yourself (an impossible task) in trying to prevent others' mistakes. While they sit in the bleachers, you play the game for them. You must make the transition to manager by becoming a coach and a trainer in the rudiments, and then you must turn the game over to them. Each must get his turn at bat to perceive, design, program, and implement. No one worth his salt wants to get stuck on maintenance jobs forever. They would rather be overloaded and told to rewrite the entire system. Personal pride and challenge are the keys.

Quality people will be increasingly difficult to find, and you must plan your turnover so that you know who is leaving and when. If you can help them leave for a better job, they will help you find good replacements. Keep in contact with other shops similar to your own and allow your people go in return for taking good people from the other shop. That way every one can gain something of a new experience. Work can even be farmed out and various packages shared so that the wheel doesn't have to be invented over and over again. Your staff will be a reflection of yourself. If they respect you, it is probably better than if they like you. You cannot be one of the boys and also lead. You will have to be able to attract, develop, control, and promote people from within to build what you need to support the company mission with DP. It is not a simple matter to have a strong ego and yet realize you will make many "people mistakes" in staffing.

Twenty percent of your staff will always carry the other 80 percent, but the 80 percent contain another 20 percent who are preparing for the future. You must know your people's strengths and, just as important, their weaknesses. You can always ask the impossible, but you must reward the practical. You must protect their health and well-being from the frequent enthusiastic demands of highly charged managements.

You must be attentive about not leaving anyone in one position too long. Frequent rotation provides the staff with a breath of fresh air and is an excellent way to back up your critical high-maintenance areas. You cannot afford to let one person become a prima donna in any one area.

Keeping your staff very busy at meaningful work is probably your best strategy for preserving overall morale. Maintaining a "freedom to leave" atmosphere with best regards and good luck will be your finest attribute.

A DP manager with no technical knowledge of what his people are doing.

Staff turnover will be your biggest problem, the one thing you can count on. You will always be searching for high-quality people. It will occupy 50 percent of your time.

POLITICS

Your politics can determine whether you move up or down. It always seems funny to hear DP professional claim he or she is not involved in politics. No one escapes politics. Politics is everywhere, from the water cooler to the boardroom. Everytime you talk to your boss, peers, users, staff, or vendors, politics prevails. You cannot prevent people from talking to people about other people. Every action you take elicits a reaction in others. Every stand you take is met by another's position.

Politics may be governed by your ego, dedication to perfection, or simply liking one person better than another. You may be aggressive, others passive, or vice versa. You have to know yourself if you would be a good politician—and then you must know people. You might as well know now that DP-ers are part of the political world too. You would be surprised at how few DP professionals really know how to read the signs. Because they spend long years concentrating on learning technology, DP professionals often find that people and communications become problems. Machines do as they are told, people don't. People say they will do one thing, then do another. Machines typically do not change their mind. Your reaction to people will affect your performance in various ways, depending on whom you are with.

One piece of political advice is to treat all people with respect. Bear in mind that anyone may be responsible for getting you fired, and they might just do it.

Fairness and honesty rank high in the world of politics. We are in an era of middle ground, where those who go too far in any direction do not survive in the political scheme of things. Yet, to change to a new system you must take a position and win.

Your attitude toward politics may come into play when you implement a new system. If you know what makes your system users tick, then you are a step ahead. An EDP executive told me once that one of the biggest political mistakes DP professionals make is that they do not become indebted to anyone. Typically, the DP-er gives and other members of the company receive, whether they like it or not.

Each outright "gift" may receive a thank-you, but it breeds resentment based on the feeling of incompetency engendered, or on being told what to do. The natural reaction is to show you something you didn't think of. Few DP professionals understand user participation and its political repercussions. For every gift an equal gift in return is the rule of politics.

If you give instruction, you must receive or allow yourself to be given instructions from the receiver. In fact, if you owe others they will keep you healthy in order to collect, very similar to banks that own a part of some businesses and are very supportive with loans.

In summary, when you are at the top of the EDP pyramid everyone is important: your boss, your peers, your staff, and outside contacts. I wonder how many DP managers have been done in by the boss's secretary—or in fact his own.

YOUR IMAGE

Your image is closely tied to your politics but is, nonetheless, a separate category in your upward progression. Different people in your organization will see you from varying points of view. Each affects the other.

If you could see yourself on TV in your own work environment, it might be very painful.

Physical characteristics such as tall or short, fat or slim, hairy or bald, smiles or frowns, are what you are to many in your organization. At the top, you are exposed as never before. People you will never know comment about you on the basis of what they see, like, and dislike. A VP of finance was confiding in his secretary one day about promoting a DP manager to director. She responded, "I guess he's okay but wouldn't you think he would cut those hairs growing out of his ears? I don't think he has the image we need." He got the job anyway, but I wonder how many people really lose on physical characteristics. Some research shows that many leaders are typically taller than average and tend to dominate interpersonal relationships more easily than smaller people. The classic all-American look clearly gets you further than other looks. If you don't have it, you will simply have to be better in other things than your competition. Everyone can be well groomed if they choose to be.

Many DP professionals have developed some careless speech habits. They are burdened with bit-and-bite talk. Except when it has something to do with files, access methods, or telecommunications, their speech is awkward and just plain stupid. What you say and how you say it makes all the difference at the top. Millions of dollars are spent in writing speeches for others to deliver, but speaking effectively is one of the more complex human tasks.

It is better to say nothing than to be known as a quick, flippant comment artist. Think before you answer. Listen before you volunteer your ideas. Never fire both barrels at once. Always keep your backup shot.

You may think it is clever or in good taste to talk like one of the country folks, but it seldom really pays off unless you are on TV. Some compulsive types comment on everything going on in the office, from tight dresses to the remarks of others. Try to keep your conversation on the business and minimize small talk.

At the top, you will find management much more aware of what they say, to whom they say it, when they say it, and in what tone of voice. Communication at the top is a system unto itself. Those who speak softly and slowly usually get heard, because so many don't exercise restraint.

Your dress is important because it tells everyone what you think of yourself and what you want to be. At the top, even in EDP, progressive, conservative, well-fitting clothes can dispel the idea that you are only a technician. If you run around in baggy pants and wear a sweater to show you are one of the hard-working DP types, you will not get invited to the boardroom. Your staff may like the rebel look, but senior management will simply ignore you. If you want to fly with the eagles, you had better look like one all of the time. You can never tell when you will be called in by the CEO to show him your plans or when he will simply decide to come over and see what's going on in the DP area. His image must be yours.

You may not think your residence is of much importance, but it can, like your dress, reflect what you think of yourself and what you want to be. Your residence must reflect where you are. Consider the $50,000-a-year executive who occupies a third-floor apartment in a ghetto area of the city. What do you think is going on? When promotion time comes, management clearly investigates the behavior of its major executives. You may say its none of their business, and it may not be. Any kind of deviant behavior, however, will attract attention when you are getting near the top. If you are living significantly above or below your means, you will be questioned. A new Rolls-Royce every year will be just as suspect as driving to work in a 1932 Ford, even if it is an antique automobile.

By the time you become a DP executive you may be approaching middle age. Your behavior may be well established or you may be feeling changes due to the pressures of upward mobility. These pressures may affect your behavior in a number of ways. Your behavior is one of the quickest ways for your management to evaluate you as promotable or for you to destroy yourself.

When you are coming up the DP pyramid, social amenities were not that important, but near the top your bearing, attitude, and performance under pressure will determine whether you go on and reap the benefit of the long years as a technical person or stay at the functional level—or worse, start the descent down the pyramid.

If you have the control to balance your behavior and to be comfortable and self-assured in social as well as business situations, you can move upward. If you do not clearly have yourself in control, you may find others talking about your behavior to management.

In our age of booze, office affairs, drugs, divorces, gambling, bribery, theft, and physical and mental illnesses, it is not unlikely to assume that you may not be able to maintain the poise to stay on top and to keep moving. Whatever problems you may encounter, your DP performance will be affected and noticed by your boss, peers, or staff. Your image can then suffer.

One of the most important aspects of image is to keep your problems out of the business environment at all costs. Confiding in people you work with is the most dangerous type of comfort.

Frequently, people want to know (innocently enough) what you did last weekend. If you told them they might be shocked. Tell them you had a nice time with your family, engaged in an acceptable sport, or took part in a church event. Golf, tennis, football, and prayer meetings build image. If you tell them you took your neighbor's wife to New York, you will be the talk of the company, whether you did or not. What you tell people makes the image difference. Don't believe they really care, because they all have their own problems.

Many DP professionals do not have a clear idea of what their image is, why it's important, or whether they even have one. The most important part of developing a personal image is having a clear focus on what you want to be. Certainly you know what you want others to think of you and perhaps what you think of yourself, but subconsciously you know what you are. You can be what you want to be. What you want to be is what you become. It sets the stage for what you do.

Your image must fit that of the company or you are finished, no matter how good you may be technically. When you move into a higher DP level, managements immediately inquire into your image.

PERSONAL DEVELOPMENT

Every day I am amazed at the number of candidates for jobs who are bewildered by the fact they have to take a step backward to spring forward again. Many professional DP people fail to see that they have progressed very quickly to the top and have achieved top salaries compared to other professionals. If they fail to keep climbing at the same rate, they think something is wrong with the company. The truth of the matter is that computer science careers accelerate quickly after the trainee phase, but then the pyramid narrows quickly. After all, one DP director supports a development manager, an operations manager and a technical manager. Since many of the professionals in these positions are relatively young, they have not developed themselves to go further. You can be stuck literally for years waiting for reorganization, termination, or foul-up at one of these levels.

Quite a few larger companies are beginning to notice that many DP professionals are, in fact, only technicians. Company managements expect the rapidly promoted DP-er to take hold in business perception and knowledge. Schools are being blamed for turning out computer science graduates who cannot comprehend an industry or its problems. The computer science graduates want to step into DP management positions on the basis of their degree alone and because they wrote 52 classroom-type programs in three languages on the school's (frequently obsolete) computer. The computer science degree is a myth and is no better than a two-year associate degree in computer programming, if the student has not combined computer skills with some basic industry business knowledge and appropriate skills such as accounting, industrial or mechanical engineering, marketing, and so forth. It is not enough to understand how computers work unless you can learn what has to be done and why they should be used. The dilemma in DP management is that technological change requires continuous relearning of technical skills and at the same time complete understanding of many other aspects of industry business operations.

By the time you reach the DP management level you are rubbing shoulders with peers who are generalists and specialists in their own fields, and they expect you to have as wide a range of knowledge as they have, as well as computer know-how. After all, you are telling them how things can and should be changed.

Personal development must take on a whole new dimension in order for you to keep up in DP management. This development is difficult to acquire after putting in 10 to 14 hours (typical) a day getting your projects implemented. Evening, graduate, or undergraduate courses are frequently a good way to continue your education and to keep from going stale. If you are career-oriented, it beats two hours of TV shows nightly. Another source of continual improvement is research in your field. Writing articles for your area of interest (preferably your company business) will keep you keyed in to new developments. Articles are relatively easy to get published. Specialized seminars such as those given by the American Management Association (AMA) will also help. Correspondence with management people in your industry will help you to know what is happening.

By all means read the trade journals of your industry, and those of specialty-related professions such as the *Journal of Accountancy.*

Self-improvement takes many forms. One of the most effective for you is public speaking (in your area of expertise). This activity will significantly improve your communications skills, increase your self-confidence, and get you a little notoriety with your own management and other company contacts. Most of all, speaking and writing will help you to organize yourself and your ideas.

If you are not active in at least one outside organization, you should ask yourself why not? I can't think of one DP pyramid head who only works a nine-to-five job, who can't be replaced overnight by an equally competent person at less money. As recessions come and go and company managements change, more and more highly paid DP managers are finding themselves "on the street." Some think it is a relatively easy task to find another equivalent job down the block. Wrong. They don't understand the job market until the unemployment checks stop. Eighty percent of terminated DP executives are still looking after eight months. Many must end up taking lesser jobs in lower job classifications. Why? Because in DP management it is up or out.

Their personal improvement has failed to keep up with what is required for DP management. You simply must acquire a host of non-DP skills to remain marketable, even in your present company. To hold your own in DP management, you have to know what is going on in company long-range business planning, so you can couple long-range DP planning to it in a meaningful way. If you have no idea of who George A. Steiner is, you had better find out.

ELECTRONIC DATA PROCESSING PLANNING

There is little question that once you have reached the top of the DP hierarchy, you will have still another challenge your predecessor did not face. Initially, data processing managers were concerned with automating certain parts of the business applications and then overseeing them in operation. As operations grew, new technology brought about the need to manage a more complex technical environment in both hardware and its associated operating software. The in-house technical support activity was born. Data base and on-line technology were introduced, and the DP pyramid head engaged in another conversion to improve the data entry and inquiry functions to a yet higher level of technology. In short, improvements in technology were driving progress, and the DP head was their implementer. It was more of the same, but with new technology. Each successive change cost companies millions of dollars in personnel and implementation costs. Few conversions could claim any significant improvement in business strategy, but they could in some cases lead to improvements in the operations of the same functions, and at lower cost. Some projects were never justified on the basis of cash, but rather only on that of being current in computerland.

The computerization of America is now on the threshold of a new conversion, only this time it is not concerned with rearranging the functions. This time it involves giving management the ability to adjust the rules of its business operation to meet the rapidly changing environment.

When you approach the middle executive level you will find that you must wear one more hat. No longer will you lead just data input, computer operations, technical support, systems development and programming. Now you will have to control systems planning, a whole new activity unto itself. Systems planning requires the following:

1 An intimate knowledge of the company business
2 A full perspective on company objectives and goals
3 A detailed understanding of all of the business applications
4 A full comprehension of the rule variables of each business application
5 A knowledge of all current DP functions and their interfaces
6 An ability to perceive what information and rule change capability and business action is required by all levels of management of the company, and why
7 An ability to perceive what functional changes in the operational system flow are needed to produce the data required

No longer will EDP be part of just the company financial empire; rather, it will be an integral part of the strategic planning for all company operations. Clearly, the era has arrived of the new DP pyramid head who is part of the senior management of the company.

A whole new plateau of perception and planning will be required to create the future computerized systems of most companies. The next conversion will involve shifting of gears, not just giving more gas. It will affect the total company, not just a department or two. The plans will focus on the following:

1 The way people do things, computer control of machines and data entry, editing, and validation
2 Information structure for different levels of management; its timing and sequence, by location
3 Data processing technological economics by location, in terms of distance
4 Management decisions and role variations, development, operational, technical support, perogatives at local and remote sites

Clearly you will have to interact with all of the top management of a company. If you do not have the moxie to perceive correctly what your company needs, sell your ideas, and interact with top management, you are finished.

Do you think you are up for all of this?

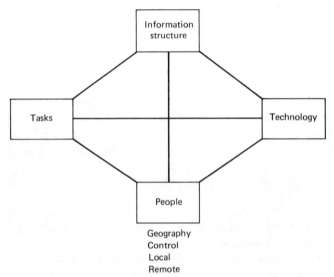

Geography
Control
Local
Remote

Figure 8-1   Business requirements and EDP planning

PERFORMANCE MEASUREMENT

At the top of the DP pyramid you will be judged on how you make use of your resources, hardware, people, and personal time.

One of the major pitfalls in DP management is playing the role of the good guy. You may agree to every hair-brained user request, put it in the stack, and produce it nine months later, sometimes after the initiator has left the company. The real error is believing that volume is a sign of productivity. Avoidance of nonmeaningful tasks is probably a better measure of productivity. Don't be afraid to say no. Another fallacy is that programmers can make up work on overtime. About the only thing accomplished is that time and a half is paid for a programmer working at 5-percent efficiency. After a straight eight hours, most programmers are making more errors than they are fixing.

Limiting the breadth of assignments will get more accomplished in the long run, from system design to coding and implementation. Users typically want everything or nothing at all. Consequently, more time and meetings are spent dealing with millions of factors that are irrelevant to the goal at hand. Your people are sitting around in meetings listening to others expound on factors not even related to current problems. The bigger the group, the lower the productivity.

Most DP productivity is realized by the assignment of overqualified staff to simple tasks. Clearly, a highly qualified and experienced person can produce more than can three trainees, with fewer errors at half the cost. Of course, if you are in the staff training business it may not matter, but training is better done on low-priority, noncritical tasks. Nothing is more ridiculous than three top professionals waiting for a trainee to finish getting an interface program completed.

By all means make your staff productive. Give them programming standards, program files, and any other devices that can tool up your shop for productivity. Don't forget good software package tools.

At the top you will be remembered for getting things done in a hurry, not for explanations of how tough the job is.

Productivity will always be improved if your shop has productivity measurements by which everyone can monitor their own performance and which you can tell management about. A few such items would be CPU utilization; job volumes; file utilizations; numbers of items processed; lines of debugged code produced; schedules met; and so forth. Keep your staff aware and you have a basis for obtaining their salary increases as well as your own.

Since you have only a finite amount of time you cannot afford to be isolated from your boss, peers, users, or staff. Therefore your personal time is important. To be effective you must learn to delegate quickly. Don't be afraid to let one of your technical programmers read a technical bulletin and give you a two-minute précis. Your staff will respond well to doing some of your work for you. Shift some of the work for requirements manuals onto users; it will make things much more specific and your staff will spend a lot less time arguing about what the user wants.

Avoid writing memorandums to anyone. Call them on the phone. Avoid the PYA (protect your analysis) game or getting them in writing. If you need help call your boss, or the user's boss and explain what you need help on: garner personal support. If you must write a memorandum, issue status reports with responsibility clearly established with dates. FYI notes are as effective handwritten as typed and they are a personal approach.

Avoid letting people tie you up in meetings. Don't let them waste your time. You might even get home to your family once in a while on time.

Insist on quality work but not perfection. Eighty percent of your work is accomplished in twenty percent of the time. The remaining twenty percent of the work usually takes eighty percent of the time. If you are going to go over each program with a fine-tooth comb, you are wasting your time and that of the initiator.

So much for performance measurement. At the top of the DP department you simply have more things to do because you have to cover more bases. You must be concerned more with how to be productive and how to get your staff productive. You need time to plan and be constantly looking for new talent.

If you can demonstrate that you are productive and can organize your staff efficiently, you will be earmarked for company activities beyond the DP area.

PROMOTIONS AT THE TOP

After you reach the top of the DP pyramid, you may ask yourself, "Where do I go from here with my life?" Whether you are in a small or a large company, you will have a choice if you have survived and have a plan. In a small company, the problem will be salary and the rate of change and expansion. You may lack a degree or the proper credentials even to get a higher position where you are. Many DP managers, through fear or plain laziness, elect to ride it out or engage in a few outside business ventures. They deserve what they get from then on.

In a large growth company, the power push from below and the sides demands that you be able to move at least laterally to other positions. But remember, what worked yesterday does not work tomorrow in DP.

Getting promoted to a job outside of data processing means that you are competing with people who are as much specialists in their field as you are in yours. Clearly, you have to be careful that some of your past experience actually does qualify you for the job. You must also be alert to the very real possibility that you could be on your way out of the company. Management may feel that you have served your purpose and they need a new kind of person so they give you a meaningless promotional or lateral job. You would be surprised how many DP managers are unable to observe this very clear signal. Some companies are very reluctant to tell a longer-term person that their services are no longer required. This policy is one of the cruelist of crimes. Conversely, the company may actually be expanding in all areas and want to give you broadening experience across many business lines. Don't hesitate to take it. Titles and the overall level of data processing may be upgraded while you are in office. Nothing could be better for your career. Take the promotion.

It is not beyond your scope to volunteer to run other departments when someone has left. Frequently reorganizations take place when a key person leaves the company. You can build your empire like everyone else. Surprisingly, DP leaders do not often think of being operating heads of other departments or incorporating other department functions into DP operations, even when those departments are highly automated. If your timing is right and management is in a bind, they may welcome your volunteer suggestion as one more thing they don't have to worry about. It is also a great way to control a good number two man under you who is pushing or perhaps overshadowing you with his capability.

Frequently your number two man is very good. After all, you trained him. You know it, he knows it, and management knows it. Now you have to do something or you become vulnerable, even if he is one of the nicest guys in the world. Sit on this problem long enough and you lose. Suppress it and you will be damaged. He will leave or you will be lateraled. You must push your people up. Become known as a developer of people and you win. They will be your best supporters in the company.

In DP-land, promotions frequently depend on the avoidance of major blunders. Current operations is your first priority, because if you can't keep your shop running, you can't do anything else. Let a few payrolls be late, miss balancing month end reports, or produce a few inaccurate inventory reports, and it's all over; even if one of your staff is to blame, it's your responsibility. You had better have the operational shop well oiled and backed up. Management will forgive you for not being too perceptive in developmental areas, but never for an ineffective shop. If you came up through computer operations you are probably fairly adept at "preventive defense." If your major claim to fame has been in systems development, you may find the fun is over when you must spend a lot of time running the DP operation. It may be difficult to give another the responsibility of developing new systems for which your experience highly qualifies you or which are your first love. As was mentioned previously, you have to give your peers some simple helpful new systems on a continuous basis to be regarded as a producer. In the large company, EDP planning is the place to be if you are a good navigator. Get them lost, however, and you regress to another company.

If you thought your career planning ended when you got to the top of the DP pyramid, you were wrong. It has just begun, and it is now much more difficult because the way has narrowed and the competition has increased.

Someone once said that there are no dead-end jobs, only dead-end people. They usually exist together. If you stay in a job over three years, you may find it impossible to go anywhere. Tom did his work, got an MBA, got involved in community affairs, lived a good life, and managed a small shop for eight years. Now, at the age of forty, he expects to find a much better job, in the same community, doing what he has been doing. The company is stable. He is restless, and a 5-percent increase in salary every two years can't do it for him. Nepotism prevails and he is stuck. Guess who is being groomed for his job—the owner's son, who just got his computer science degree. Tom is in trouble. Tom didn't plan beyond his present DP manager job.

PREPARE FOR YOUR TERMINATION

After you are in a DP management role you may become aware of the peril of terminations. When you are younger you are allowed a few mistakes. Data processing job changes are very acceptable in computerland. At the management level you are allowed fewer mistakes, if any. The setbacks can ruin you. Clearly, you are entitled to change jobs when you are improving yourself, but there comes the time when you are pegged as a job jumper, real or perceived. You may be able to explain clearly what happened in each case. The question is whether you will ever get the chance to explain before you go over the hill. The suspicion exists that something is wrong with you. Employers think your short stays will continue with them. They bypass your interview. Each job change should move you along your career path on schedule. The plan must commence when you have just attained your management position. When you have been unexpectedly terminated is no time to start the plan, because you are in too much of a state of shock to do anything effectively. You may end up having to accept a poorer job at a remote location, doing anything, including programming, just to feed the kids and meet living expenses. You may have to draw on your savings and spend months in a job search. It happens frequently to DP managers too. You may not recover. You really have to go through it all before you appreciate the psychological and fiscal complications. Terminated DP managers are difficult to place and have a lot of competition.

Terminations are categorized as voluntary and involuntary. If you have done your DP career planning homework, you clearly know where you are going and why. Good DP managers are always looking and investigating what is going on in the job market. They have no problem letting their management and sometimes their staff know that they are always getting calls for other jobs. It helps to disarm everyone that they are not really looking and that their company loyalty is intact. If once you decide to look, it then causes very little attention: obviously, if you had wanted to leave, you would have done so.

Sometimes opportunity only knocks once. If the door is not opened, it goes away. If your plan is complete, you know the next job when you see it. If the timing is right, you leap to the top of a bigger pyramid. Probably a hundred factors are involved in such a decision. There are many trade-offs, and no job is perfect.

Leaving the DP management of a company involves many more complications than merely giving two-weeks' notice. Management will want to know why. Psychologically, your departure can affect other managers, the status of projects, the endorsement of plans, and surely your staff and boss. It is no light matter. They will want to know all about your new job. Limit these discussions.

Leaving requires assurances that they are a good company, that all is well, and that it has been a hard decision for you. Seldom is the truth accepted. There are always some who assume that some complaint you had in the past is the reason. Someone is always trying to pin it on someone or something in the company.

Even if you have complaints, don't voice one of them. Management references will be needed in the future. You must protect yourself at all costs. If you torpedo someone on the way out, it will always get you in the future. Never try to name your successor; that's management's prerogative. Offer to leave immediately—to your boss. He should be the first to know, not your staff. Let your boss know right off that you want no counteroffers and the decision is final. A clean break is essential. Of course, your boss is never the reason . . . even if he is. Terminate with poise and a touch of class. Be willing to provide the transition for your replacement. Show that you are ethical by finishing up any uncompleted work.

The other type of termination can be the biggest shock in your life, if you are not prepared for it. A company may gently tell you to take your time or they may clear you out in ten minutes, usually Friday night at 4:50 P.M. You may have an inkling it's coming through a warning, or you may not.

In either case, you've been fired. They will seldom tell you the real reason: it is probably many reasons, and who really wants to get into them anyway? It's too late. What counts is how they are going to respond to your reference checks. Today, there are many laws regarding terminations, and most major companies know them because the lawsuits cost millions of dollars a year and tape recorders on phones are used to prove what is said regarding terminations.

Be sure you get it straight on how the reference check will address the following:

Quality of your work
Chemistry between you and your boss
Your management strengths

Your technical strengths

Your integrity and personal relationships

The reason for your termination

Agreement that nothing else will be volunteered, such as weaknesses

When you have been fired you have some bargaining power on these items. Some DP managers, in a state of shock, simply fail to get concessions and jeopardize their entire future by not knowing what to ask for.

If you are a good bargainer, you may be able to get some of the following, but don't count on it.

An office relay phone to your home to answer job calls

A continuance of employment pay to seek another job

Severance pay to tide you over

A good recommendation in writing

An office to serve as a base for your job search

An out-placement consulting service to help you get another job

Above all, don't panic. Treat a firing just the same as if you had voluntarily terminated, and start your job search the next day. If you dwell on it, you lose.

The one great thing about DP is that there is a large demand for DP talent of all kinds.

SUMMARY

The purpose of this chapter is to alert you to what you will be faced with if you achieve your goal of reaching the top of the DP pyramid. Career planning never really stops. It is even more critical when you achieve DP management positions, because you have invested so much and stand to lose it all. Sometimes events are totally beyond your control. Your hopes and anticipation can turn to fatigue and disillusionment regarding companies and, worse, to disappointment in yourself. Was it an impossible goal in the first place, or were you simply not up to it? As in the political world, there are some winners and some losers. The important thing is that you tried. Even the winners stop and wonder what they have attained and know not where the next landslide will bring them.

There is a point at which all finally reach the last rung of progress. That one last résumé reflects what you finally did in DP that's worth mentioning.

Nine

Make the Most of Future Developments in Data Processing

A new era is beginning for the DP professional. The demand for intelligent, skilled, motivated, creative, and personable DP people has far surpassed any foreseeable supply.

TECHNOLOGY

Computer hardware costs have decreased significantly and will probably continue to decrease as technology advances. More complex computer software will continue to be developed that will allow those with little training to create their own personal programs using data bases and communications techniques developed by more technical DP professionals. Clearly, low-cost, intelligent, data-entry display devices will help to prevent erroneous data from entering the data banks. More people with less training will utilize central files, a situation exemplified by terminals used in banks to disburse cash. "On-line systems are the future," were Dick Sprague's words in 1965. A larger gap will open between technical specialists and applications programmers.

There are those who suggest that users will be given the software-report-generation capability to bypass the programmer analyst and interface directly with the computer. In a few years anyone who does not have a working knowledge of computers will be considered uneducated. The challenge will shift to preventing every Tom, Dick, and Mary from generating millions of meaningless reports simply because the computer terminal is available. More time can be spent playing with the computer than thinking about or doing the job they were hired for.

DATA PROCESSING PERSONNEL

Salaries for qualified DP professionals will continue to skyrocket through the 1980s. It appears that standards for productivity will be increasingly applied to DP work, by means of structured top-down programming, design standards and project control methods. Mediocrity will always seek safety in standardization. Standardization may get more efficient volume, but seldom creates a quantum jump. Creativity and change seldom deal with the whys of the past, rather with a shift in perspective for the future. Those people with a variety of experience will stand out and surpass those with greater in-depth experience in limited business application areas. As salary discrepancies occur, the movement of DP professionals will become greater and job mobility as a way of life will become even more pronounced.

Politics will still play an important role in progress up the DP pyramid. Those who plan their careers and get just the right depth and types of experience will move quickly through the crowd of nonprofessionals. It is not necessarily to your advantage to try to get into management too quickly while you can continue to move up in systems, programming, or operations.

It is highly unlikely that top managements will ever understand the DP dilemmas that occur because of management's changing objectives and goals. Some companies have spent millions in large DP fiascos in centralizing the company data base only to have it collapse under its own weight. Technology moved so quickly that decentralization and distributed processing became more economical and useful to those who were responsible for the profits of the business. One conversion after another took place with very little value added to recover the investment. Technology frequently created an inflexible system that could not easily respond when a whole new approach could have saved millions of dollars.

Many computerworld high priests and hardware/software experts, in the interest of keeping up with technology, are blind to good business sense. Unneeded tools are created and purchased to satisfy the thirst to be first. Business rules are programmed in the computer and imposed on operating managers until they are frustrated by the complex system they are supposed to control. Thinking stops and the same functions and rules continue. Those at the top of the pyramid will be replaced more quickly than ever before, if management perceives they are not able to change the system to meet business needs and manage the new breed of DP professionals effectively.

Continuing educational and personal knowledge development will become an absolute necessity. Users will have just enough knowledge of what the computer can do and how to make it more difficult to hide behind a thicket of buzzwords and acronyms as an excuse for nonperformance.

Clearly, larger companies will continue to attract a majority of qualified DP people and will limit or dehumanize them in narrow job classifications with salary levels and specialized training. Smaller companies will be required to follow suit, but owing to their lack of selection expertise and lower training budgets, they will probably get less productivity for the dollar spent and experience greater turnover.

Some alert companies will realize that their DP staff can actually be improved by having fewer but better-qualified, highly paid staff, and by using part-time services of highly qualified independents.

Some slow-witted companies will continue to pay exorbitant rates for packages or for outsiders to do all of the programming required for their system. Small specialized programming houses will flourish and will train their junior people at the expense of these small companies.

In each of the above cases, the most that can be accomplished is for one company to take from another. As the DP personnel and software budgets approach 75 percent of all EDP spending, senior company managements will insist on greater productivity from their EDP pyramid head but will be unable to understand how this can be accomplished. Just as large companies have realized the economics of farming out up to 25 percent of their computer processing and of utilizing temporary help to meet peak loads during volume seasons, the DP head may undertake his computer program development using a few top-grade professionals of other companies on a part-time basis for the coding phase of system development.

Computer system analysts and programmers with talent in specific business applications, hardware, and software will work evenings and weekends for other employers, effectively increasing the supply of scarce talent, and enhancing their own experience base. The basic company fear of using outside individual contractors will vanish under the pressure for quicker results. Standards for systems and programming documentation will be the rule. Packaged application software will abound, even from accounting firms, who will be paid for the programs and the privilege of auditing their own work.

Electronic data processing software agents will emerge in the unique position of middlemen, managing data bases of talent capabilities among companies so that there is little, if any, waiting time between program development and the acquisition of temporary talent. As it is with unions, you will register with a temporary agency data bank of professional skills that are on call for many companies. Standards of performance will be more predominant.

What does this mean for you, the DP professional? If you want to become one of the best, you must know your job extremely well so that every job you undertake gets five stars. You will have the opportunity to move up as fast as you can develop your business and technical talent. You will be able to earn as much or more than any other professional, if you are talented and motivated. When you are ready for the next position, you will simply go and find it.

You must take advantage of your training and knowledge quickly. The systems and programs you develop will be used by others, who will rise up their company organization because of your efforts. They may even resist the changes you bring about in their work life. In the end, you will be forgotten for the good work you do today. Your work will be tomorrow's yesterday and the most you can really hope for is to die in your sleep. Can anyone even remember who designed the great bridges and buildings they see today? What counts is who owns them.

There are no guarantees of success in data processing. It is probably still more gratifying to be a captain of a tugboat than the engineering room officer of the biggest ship afloat, although no one is always master of his fate.

You, the DP professional, are changing the way companies are doing business. If you think your career will automatically be assured when you can spell COBOL, you are wrong. In fact, the pace will become more frantic until you finally rise to your level of incompetence and finally revert to the activities you perform well. When you finally complete your DP career, you may look back and wonder if all those long hours, successes, and fiascos were worth it. They certainly are because you will have had a role in one of the greatest advances of our time. As the oil crisis continues, data processing will be one of the key industries in the revival of American productivity. If the workers cannot economically go to work, the work will be brought to them through computer power and communications techniques. Homework stations are possible, but they give rise to a whole new set of problems.

Applications software development (on-line) is the future and you are its catalyst. There are not enough DP specialists to fill the demand. When the situation happened in the telephone industry not long ago, it seemed that everyone in the United States would have to be converted into a switchboard operator to handle the number of calls. Then some ingenious programmer invented the automatic self-dial system. Look for a similar breakthrough in programming using more complex DP software tools.

YOUR FUTURE

The trends are there for you to observe.

Computer hardware prices are going down relative to computational performance (see Figure 9-1). Overall DP costs are headed up owing to the cost of labor, inflation, and the shortage of talent (see Figure 9-2).

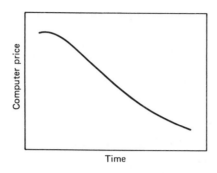

Figure 9-1   Computer hardware prices.

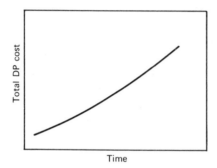

Figure 9-2   Total DP costs.

The purchases of operating, utility, data base, communication, data retrieval, graphic, resource accounting, and programming tools and business application software are headed upward, and this increases programming productivity (see Figure 9-3).

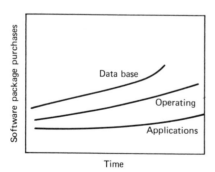

Figure 9-3   Software purchases.

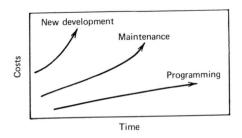

Figure 9-4   Development, maintenance and programming costs.

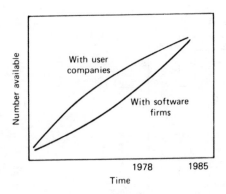

Figure 9-5   Programmer employment.

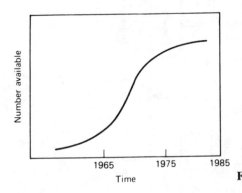

Figure 9-6   Programmer population.

The evolution of data processing has progressed from simple to more
complex functions in phases, roughly as follows:

Phase I—1960s   Single-phase application programs
                     Multiple concurrent operation programs
                     More complex operating software

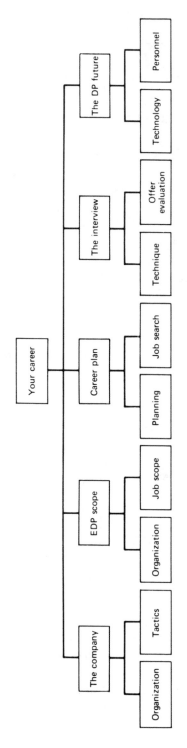

Figure 9-7 Top-down DP career planning.

Phase II—1970s	Data base software for application programs
	Data communications and on-line software
	Data retrieval software
	Programming aid software
	Business application software
Phase III—1980s	Integration of data base, communication, and on-line software from single software vendors
	End-point user-terminal service control, prompting, and decision-making inquiry response (action) capability (i.e., airline reservation system)
Phase IV—1990s	Integration of "variable-rule" on-line business application package software, to allow support and flexibility for fast-changing business conditions and goals, tied to data base on-line software
	More simplified programmer aids and user-oriented languages
	More preprogrammed question/answer guidance, correlation, and usage software for application data bases

SUMMARY

So there you have it.

Congratulations on choosing to be a DP professional on the frontier of the future computerworld. Develop your detail résumé to the fullest and use it to achieve success. If you reach the top of the EDP pyramid you will know how the DP mind works and how to find the best DP professionals available.

Good luck to you in your DP career. Success is a journey, not a destination. You will realize that the more things change the more they remain the same.

Our last computer conversation convinced us. We would
like you to transform our entire operation into a
totally manual system. Our objectives include becoming
the largest employer in town, having lots of operational
backup, providing for a base of creativity, and elimi-
nating hardware, software, and DP staff costs.

Electronic Data Processing Organizations

AFIPS	American Federation of Information Processing Societies
DPMA	Data Processing Management Association
ACM	Association for Computing Machinery
CLA	Computer Law Association
EAF	EDP Auditors Foundation
ADAPSO	Association of Data Processing Organizations
AEDS	Association of Educational Data Systems
IEEE	Institute for Electrical and Electronic Engineers
IIA	Information Industry Association
MITA	Microcomputer Industry Trade Association
ASM	Association for Systems Management
URISA	Urban and Regional Information Systems Association
NAIS	National Association of State Information Associations
IDCMA	Independent Data Communications Manufacturers

System Software Suppliers by Package Type

Application System Development
Applied Data Research, Inc.
CACI
CAP-CPP, Inc.
Decision Strategy Corp.
IBM
Informatics, Inc.
Information Builders, Inc.
M. Bryce and Associates
Programart

Data Base Management
Applied Data Research, Inc.
Cincom Systems, Inc.
Computer Corp. of America
Cullinane Corp.
Infodata Systems, Inc.
IBM
International Data Base Systems, Inc.
Intel Corp. (MRI Division)
Mathematica, Inc., Products Group
MSP, Inc.
Software AG of North America
Synergetics Corp.
University Computing Co.

Data Communications Control
Altergo Software, Inc.
Applied Data Research, Inc.
Boole & Babbage, Inc.
Cincom Systems, Inc.

Comm-Pro Associates
IBM
Intel Corp. (MRI Division)
Kranzely & Co.
Mathematica, Inc., Products Group
SDA Products, Inc.
Software AG of North America
Turnkey Systems, Inc.
Western Electric Co.
Westinghouse Electric Corp.

Computer Graphics
California Computer Products Inc. (CalComp)
Decision Graphics
Environmental Systems Research Institute
Escape Ltd.
IBM
Integrated Software Systems Corp.
Laboratory for Computer Graphics and Spatial Analysis
Structural Dynamics Research Corp.
Radian Corp.

Data Center Production Control
Johnson Systems, Inc.
Systematics, Inc.
Value Computing, Inc.
University Computing Co.

Resource Accounting and Performance Evaluation
Applied Data Research, Inc.
BGS Systems, Inc.
Boeing Computer Services Co.
Boole & Babbage, Inc.
Candle Corp.
Capex Corp.
Computer Associates
Comten, Inc.
Duquesne Systems, Inc.
IBM
Johnson Systems, Inc.
Marino Associates
Performance Systems, Inc.
SDA Products, Inc.
Value Computing, Inc.
Westinghouse Electric Corp.

DASD Space Management
Allen Services Corp.
Boole & Babbage, Inc.
Cambridge Systems Group
IBM
Informatics, Inc.
Oxford Software Corp.
Pansophic Systems, Inc.
SDI
Software Module Marketing
Tower Systems, Inc.
Universal Software, Inc.
Value Computing, Inc.
Westinghouse Electric Corp.

Program Development Aids
Adpac Computing Languages Corp.
Applied Data Research, Inc.
Arkay Computer, Inc.
CAP-CPP, Inc.
Capex Corp.
CGA Computer Associates
DASD Corp.

Dataware, Inc.
Hansco Data Processing, Inc.
IBM
Informatics, Inc.
Management and Computer Services, Inc.
Micro Focus Ltd.
MSP, Inc.
Occidental Computer Systems
On-line Business Systems, Inc.
On-line Software International
University Computing Co.
Westinghouse Electric Co.

Data Retrieval, Analysis, Reporting
Applications Software, Inc.
Azrex, Inc.
Cambridge Computer Associates, Inc.
Capex Corp.
Computer Associates
Cullinane Corp.
Dataman Corp.
Dylakor Software Systems, Inc.
IBM
Informatics, Inc.
McDonnell Douglas Automation Co.
NCI
Optipro, Inc.
Pansophic Systems, Inc.
Program Products, Inc.
SAS Institute, Inc.
SDA Products, Inc.
Software International
SPSS, Inc.
System Support Software, Inc.
Systems Development Corp.

IS&R and Text Management
A.R.A.P.
Applied Data Research, Inc.
IBM

Library Management
Applied Data Research, Inc.
Capex Corp.
Goal Systems
NCI
Pansophic Systems, Inc.
SDI
Tower Systems, Inc.
University Computing Co.
Value Computing, Inc.

Operating System Enhancements
Comten, Inc.
IBM
Innovation Data Processing
Jason Data Services, Inc.
Nixdorf Computer Software Co.
University Computing Co.
Value Computing, Inc.

Application Software Vendors and Software Application Areas

American Valuation Consultants, Inc.
  Des Plaines, Il
    General accounting
    Medical administration

AM/Jacquard Systems
  Santa Monica, CA
    General accounting
    Payroll
    Word processing

Argonaut Information Systems, Inc.
  Oakland, CA
    General accounting
    Payroll

Aries Information Systems, Inc.
  Minneapolis, MN
    General accounting
    Payroll

Arthur Andersen & Co.
  Chicago, IL
    General accounting
    Manufacturing
    Medical and health care
    Sales and distribution

ASK Computer Services, Inc.
  Los Altos, CA
    General accounting
    Manufacturing

Atlantic Software, Inc.
  Philadelphia, PA
    Management sciences

The Automated Quill, Inc.
  Englewood, CO
    Construction Accounting
    General accounting
    Manufacturing

Bancroft Computer Systems, Inc.
  West Monroe, LA
    General accounting
    Graphics
    Manufacturing
    Payroll
    Word processing

Basic/Four Corp.
  Tustin, CA
    Management sciences
    Medical and health care

Baybanks Data Services, Inc.
  Waltham, MA

M. Bryce & Associates, Inc.
  Cincinnati, OH
    Performance standards

Burroughs Corp.
  Detroit, MI

CACI
  Los Angeles, CA
    Management sciences

Cado Systems Corp.
  Torrance, CA
    Auto sales accounting
    Insurance

California Computer Products, Inc.
  Anaheim, CA
    Graphic arts
Chi Corp.
  Cleveland, OH
    Mathematics and statistics
Cincom Systems, Inc.
  Cincinnati, OH
    Manufacturing
Computer Corp. of America
  Cambridge, MA
    Electronic mail
Comsery Corp.
  Minneapolis, MN
    General accounting
    Manufacturing
    Sales and distribution
Condata, Inc.
  Philadelphia, PA
    Payroll/personnel
The Continuum Co.
  Austin, TX
    Insurance
    Medical and health care
Control Data Corp.
  Minneapolis, MN 55440
Cullinane Corp.
  Wellesley, MA
    Auditing
Cyborg Systems, Inc.
  Chicago, IL
    Payroll/personnel
Data Design Associates, Inc.
  Santa Clara, CA
    General accounting
Data General Corp.
  Westboro, MA
Datapoint Corp.
  San Antonio, TX
Digital Equipment Corp.
  Maynard, MA

Disc, Inc.
  Owings Mills, MD
    Banking and finance
    General accounting
Execucom Systems Corp.
  Austin, TX
    Financial planning
Financial Systems Consultants
Division of Indiana Bank
  Fort Wayne, IN
    Banking and finance
Financial Technology, Inc.
  Chicago, IL
    Banking and finance
Finar Systems Ltd.
  New York, NY
    Financial analysis
First National Bank of Boston
  Wellesley, MA
    Stock purchases
Florida Software Services, Inc.
  Orlando, FL.
    General banking and finance
    Manufacturing
    Payroll
Fortex Data Corp.
  Chicago, IL
    General accounting
Harris-SAI, Inc.
  Ann Arbor, MI
    Electrical engineering
Haverly Systems, Inc.
  Denville, NJ
    Management sciences
    Mathematics and statistics
HBO & Co.
  Atlanta GA
    Medical and health care
Hewlett-Packard Co.
  Palo Alto, CA
Honeywell, Inc.
  Waltham, MA

IBM Data Processing Division
  White Plains, NY
IBM General Systems Division
  Atlanta, GA
Infonational
  San Diego, CA
    General accounting
Informatics, Inc.
  Canoga Park, CA
    Banking and finance
    General accounting
    Insurance
    Manufacturing
    Payroll/personnel
Information Associates, Inc.
  Rochester, NY
    Education
    General accounting
Information Science, Inc. (Insci)
  Montvale, NJ
    Payroll/personnel
Insurance Systems of America, Inc.
  Atlanta, GA
    Banking and finance
    Insurance
International Mathematical &
Statistical Libraries, Inc. (IMSL)
  Houston, TX
    Mathematics and statistics
International Systems, Inc.
  King of Prussia, PA
    Banking
    Management sciences
K & H Computer Systems, Inc.
  Sparta, NJ
    Management sciences
Kranzley & Co.
  Cherry Hill, NJ
    Banking and finance
MacNeal-Schwendier, Inc.
  Los Angeles, CA
    Engineering-construction

Management Science America, Inc.
(MSA)
  Atlanta, GA
    Banking and finance
    General accounting
    Manufacturing
    Payroll/personnel
    Tax tables
Martin Marietta Data Systems
  Towson, MD
    Management sciences
    Manufacturing
McCormack & Dodge Corp.
  Needham Heights, MA
    Banking and finance
    General accounting
    Manufacturing
McDonnell Douglas Automation Co.
  St. Louis, MO
    Engineering-construction
    Management sciences
Medical Information Technology, Inc.
  Cambridge, MA
    Electronic mail
    Medical and health care
Mini-Computer Business
Applications, Inc. (MCBA)
  Glendale, CA
    General accounting
    Manufacturing
    Sales and distribution
    Tax preparation
Modular Computer Systems, Inc.
(Modcomp)
  Fort Lauderdale, FL
    General accounting
    Payroll
NCR Corp.
  Dayton, OH
Nichols & Co.
  Culver City, CA
    Management sciences

The Office Manager, Inc.
  Seattle, WA
    General accounting
    Manufacturing
    Sales and distribution
    Word processing
Personal Software, Inc.
  Sunnyvale, CA
    Accounting
    Computer games
    Miscellaneous
Plycom Services, Inc.
  Plymouth, IN
    General accounting
    Payroll
Point 4 Data Corp.
(Formerly Educational Data
Systems)
  Irvine, CA
    General accounting
    Management sciences
    Text editing
The Poise Co., Inc.
  Roswell, NM
    Education
Policy Management Systems
  Columbia, SC
    Banking and finance
    Insurance
Price Waterhouse & Co.
  New York, NY
    Banking and finance
    General accounting
Prime Computer, Inc.
  Framingham, MA
Pritsker & Associates, Inc.
  W. Lafayette, IN
    Management sciences
    Mathematics and statistics
Program Products, Inc.
  Montvale, NJ
    Auditing

Qpac America, Inc.
  Manchester, NH
    Payroll/personnel
Resource Software International, Inc.
  Englewood Cliffs, NJ
    Banking and finance
    Education
    General accounting
    Management sciences
    Payroll/personnel
SAB, Inc.
  New York, NY
    Tax preparation/planning
St. Joseph's Bank & Trust Co.
  South Bend, IN
    Banking and finance
Software Assistance
  Santa Clara, CA
    General accounting
    Medical and health care
Software International Corp.
  Andover, MA
    General accounting
    Manufacturing
    Payroll/personnel
Sperry Univac
  Blue Bell, PA
SPSS, Inc.
  Chicago, IL
    Mathematics and statistics
Stockholder Systems, Inc.
  Atlanta, GA
    Banking and finance
    General accounting
System Research Inc.
  Okemos, MI
    Education
    General accounting
    Payroll/personnel
Systonetics, Inc.
  Anaheim, CA
    Management sciences

Technical Analysis Corp.
  Atlanta, GA
    Payroll/personnel
    Sales and distribution
    Word processing
Tektronix, Inc.
  Beaverton, OR
    Graphics design
Timberline Systems
  Beaverton, OR
    Specialized accounting systems
Time Share Corp.
  West Hartford, CT
    Education
Tymeshare Banking Systems
  Birmingham, AL
    Banking and finance
    General accounting
UCLA Health Sciences Computing
Facility
  Los Angeles, CA
    Mathematics and statistics
United Computing Systems, Inc.
Business Information Products
  Kansas City, MO
    Banking and finance
    Tax planning
University Computing Co.
  Dallas, TX
    Banking and finance
    Manufacturing

Versatek, Inc.
  Santa Clara, CA
    Plotting graphics
Wang Laboratories, Inc.
  Lowell, MA
Warrex Computer Corp.
  Richarson, TX
    Banking and finance
    General accounting
    Payroll/personnel
    Sales and distribution
Warrington Associates
  Minneapolis, MN
    Banking and finance
Weiland Computer Group, Inc.
  Oakbrook, IL
    Banking and finance
Western Electric
  Greensboro, NC
    Electrical Engineering
    Graphics design
    Mathematics and statistics
Bob White Computing & Software,
Inc.
  Naperville, IL
    Banking and finance
Wood & Tower, Inc.
  Princeton, NJ
    Construction

Manufacturing Software Vendors and Application Areas

Company Name	Product Name	Modules
American Software, Inc. Atlanta, GA	Manufacturing Management Systems	Master production schedule, capacity requirements planning, bill of material, MRP, product costing, shop floor control, purchasing
A.O. Smith Data Systems Division Brown Deer, WI	Manufacturing Data System	Cost control, engineering data control, forecasting, inventory and stores control, shop floor control, purchasing, MRP
Applied Information Development, Inc. Oak Brook, IL	AID-Manufacturing Control System (AID-MCS)	MRP, inventory management and control, capacity requirements planning, master production scheduling, purchasing control, sales forecasting, customer order control, distribution requirements planning, resource requirements planning, work-in-process control

Company Name	Product Name	Modules
Arista Manufacturing Systems, A Division of Xerox Corp. Winston-Salem, NC	Arista Manufacturing Systems	Manufacturing standards, inventory records control, historical forecasting, master production scheduling, material requirements planning, shop floor control, capacity requirements planning, tele-communications access method (on-line), cost management system, procurement management system, simulated requirements planning
Arthur Anderson & Co. Chicago, IL	MAC-PAC-RPG	Labor performance reporting, inventory control, master production schedule, MRP, shop floor control, capacity requirements planning, inventory accounting, manufacturing engineering, design engineering, product costing.
	MAC-PAC COBOL	Purchasing, inventory control, master production schedule, MRP, shop floor control, capacity requirements planning, inventory accounting, manufacturing and design engineering

Company Name	Product Name	Modules
ASK Computer Systems, Inc. Los Altos, CA	MANMAN	Inventory management and control, bill of material, MRP, purchasing, shop floor control, capacity requirements planning
Associates for Management Services, Inc. Bellevue, WA	Manufacturing, Management, and Control	Order processing, purchase order control, shop floor control, routing, bill of material, MRP, inventory
Boeing Computer Services Seattle, WA	PMS (Production Management System)	Bill of material, master scheduling, MRP, inventory control, purchase order control, optional parts, shop order control, in process control, job and standards routing, performance reporting and accounting feedback, capacity requirements planning
Bristol Information Systems, Inc. Fall River, MA	Manufacturing Systems	Manufacturing order processing, billing, perpetual inventory, bill of material, material requirements planning
Burroughs Corp. Detroit, MI	PCS III	Engineering data control, MRP, master production scheduling, work in process, operation scheduling and loading, capacity requirements planning forecasting and inventory analysis

Company Name	Product Name	Modules
Business Controls Corp. Elmwood Park, NJ	MIN-MACS (Manufacturing Inventory and Materials Control System)	Inventory control system, bill of material, purchasing, work in process, inventory control, job tracking, vendor performance analysis, MRP
Cincom Systems, Inc. Cincinnati, OH	Manufacturing Resource Planning System (MRPS)	Product control, vendor analysis and purchasing, master production scheduling, MRP, shop floor control and production planning control, bill of material
Compudata Systems, Inc. Westport, CT	Manufacturing System for IBM Series I	Bill of material, order processing, work order preparation, inventory, purchasing, sales analysis
Computer Covenant Corp. Farmington, CT	Integrated Manufacturing System	Bill of material, materials inventory, labor distribution, job costing, production scheduling
Computer Methods, Inc. Milwaukee, WI	PROFIT	Bill of material, production control and costing, MRP
Computer Systems Engineering Burlington, MA	Total Manufacturing System	Bill of material, materials requirements planning, production cost and control, inventory control, MRP, shop floor control, capacity planning
	Job Accounting System	Job costing

Company Name	Product Name	Modules
Computer Technology, Inc. Bellevue, WA	MCS (Manufacturing Control System)	Bill of material, purchase order tracking, work in process, tracking and costing, inventory control
Comserve Corp. Mendota Heights, MN	AMAPS (Advanced Manufacturing, Accounting, Production System)	Bill of material, material control, material requirements planning, purchasing control, process and routing, shop floor control, capacity requirements planning, standard casting, master production scheduling
Data Systems for Industry Long Beach, CA	COP	Customer order processing
	JCP	Job cost processing
	SFP	Shop floor processing
	MM/3000	Materials management
	Mfg/3000	Manufacturing
Data 3 Systems, Inc. Santa Rosa, CA	MRPS 34/38	Business forecasting, order entry, resource capacity planning, master production scheduling, work order management, inventory management, purchase order management, product structures, material requirements planning, detail capacity planning, shop floor control, standard product costing

Company Name	Product Name	Modules
DeBugge Computer Services East Hanover, NJ	PRO III	Sales order processing, sales forecasting, job costing, job forecasting, master scheduling engineering bill of material, purchasing (includes dock to stock). WIP control, stores control, production planning, materials requirement planning, cost accounting, physical inventory, shop floor control
Decision Sciences Corp. Jenkintown, PA	SPARS	Sales projection and requirements scheduling
Digital Business Systems, Inc. Reading, MA	Part of TAG distribution accounting system	Bill of Material MRP
Digital Equipment Corp. Merrimack, NH	LOTS (Labor and Operations Tracking System)	Complete shop floor control
EDS Compusource Corp. Dallas, TX	Distribution, Manufacturing	Inventory control, bill of material, master schedule, shop floor control, cost control, MRP
Escom, Inc. Bellevue, WA	MMC (Manufacturing Management and Control)	Engineering entry, sales order entry, inventory planning, work order launching, purchase order processing, work in process costing

Company Name	Product Name	Modules
Factory Systems Division of Rolfe Assoc. Rocky Hill, CT	TRAC 80	Shop floor control, production scheduling, work in process
Far West Data Systems Irvine, CA	MAC-PAC/HP	Design engineering, inventory control, material requirements planning, purchasing, manufacturing engineering, product costing, shop floor control, capacity requirements planning, inventory accounting, master scheduling, contract tracability
Formation, Inc. Mt. Laurel, NJ	FORMAN	MRP, capacity requirements planning, shop floor control, master prod. scheduling, purchasing, inventory control
Gaines Systems Group Oak Brook, IL	General Adaptive Inventory System	Demand forecasting, inventory management
Hewlett-Packard Cupertino, CA	Materials Management 3000	Master production schedule, bill of material, inventory management and control with purchase order tracking, purchasing, MRP, standard product costing
Honeywell Information System Waltham, MA	HMS	MRP, master production schedule, forecasting, capacity requirements planning, inventory management control, manufacturing data control

Company Name	Product Name	Modules
IBM Corp. DP Div. White Plains, NY	COPICS	Engineering and production, data control, forecasting, MPR, inventory accounting, shop floor control, capacity requirements planning, product costing
IBM Corp. General Systems Div. Atlanta, GA	IPICS	Engineering and production data control, product costing, inventory accounting, material requirements planning, capacity planning, production control
	MAPICS	Order entry, sales analysis, inventory management, product data management, material requirements planning, production control and costing, data collection system support
ICL, Inc. Distributive Systems Div. Irving, TX	Extended SAFES (Small Factory Systems)	Bill of material, costing, inventory, work in process, extended RP
Informatics, Inc. Des Plaines, IL	Manufacturing Systems	Product cost control, shop floor control, inventory control, material requirements planning
Information Management Technologies Chicago, IL	MACS	Inventory control, purchasing, job costing, MRP, engineering

Company Name	Product Name	Modules
Integral Business Computing, Inc. Harbor City, CA	Manufacturing Management System	Bill of material, WIP/job costing, inventory control, MRP, purchasing
Interactive Applications, Inc. Sunnyvale, CA	MRP Command System	Bill of material, MRP, capacity requirements planning, shop floor control
Interactive, Inc. San Diego, CA	Infoflo	Bill of material, shop orders, MRP, shop floor control, inventory control, capacity requirements planning, purchasing
Interactive Information Systems Cincinnati, OH	Interactive Management Control System	Inventory management and control, manufacturing standards, shop floor control, purchasing, MRP, bill of material, capacity requirements planning
Interactive Management Systems, Inc. Belmont, MA	MRP IMS Systems	Bill of material, shop floor control, purchasing, inventory, MRP
Jacobsen & Associates, Inc. Temple City, CA	Manufacturing Control Systems	Shop floor control, MRP, bill of material, capacity requirements planning, inventory control, WIP/job costing

Company Name	Product Name	Modules
Management Technology, Inc. Holland, MI	MIPS	Forecasting master production schedule, bill of material, MRP, shop floor control, inventory control, WIP/job costing, capacity requirements planning
Mandate Corp. Cleveland, OH	Manufacturing Management System	Production costing, MRP, inventory management, job costing, shop floor control, purchasing, product data control
Manufacturing Resources Management Milwaukee, WI	PACS	Data base planning, bill of material, data base control, master production schedule, MRP, capacity requirements planning, priority dispatching, standard costing, standard job order costing, manufacturing order—material and stock locations, manufacturing order—labor purchase order and vendor shipping or sales order
Martin-Marietta Data Systems Baltimore, MD	MAS-E	MRP, master production scheduling, shop floor control, capacity requirements planning, purchasing, cost control

Company Name	Product Name	Modules
Martin-Marietta Data Systems (continued)	MAS-II	Production control, cost control, inventory control, purchasing, business planning
	MAS-I	Same as MAS-II, plus customer order processing, master production scheduling
	MAS-H	Same as MAS-E
Metasystems, Inc. University Heights, OH	IMPACS (Interactive Manufacturing Planning and Control System)	Bill of material, inventory control, capacity and material requirements planning, production control, shop floor reporting
Mid-America Computer Corp. Bensville, IL	MACE	Production control, inventory management, shop floor control, capacity planning, MRP, bill of material, purchasing
Mitrol, an operation of General Electric Information Services Co. Burlington, MA	MIMS: Industrial Management Systems Very High Level Language (VHLL) oriented to manufacturing systems	Inventory control, engineering production control, shop floor control, capacity requirements planning, cost control, purchasing, MRP
NCA Corp. Sunnyvale, CA	Manufacturing MS-II Manufacturing System	Inventory control, bill of material, MRP, capacity requirements planning, shop floor control, purchasing

Company Name	Product Name	Modules
NCR Dayton, OH	IMCS II	Bill of material, inventory control, MRP, routing, work in process, capacity planning, order processing, sales analysis (released in July 1980), in development for 1981 release: purchase/receiving, master production scheduling
	MISSION	Bill of material, routing, costing, material management on-line, inventory management, master production scheduling, material requirements planning, capacity requirements planning, WIP, order processing, purchasing/receiving
Optimum Systems, Inc. Santa Clara, CA	Manufacturing Inventory Control System	Bill of material, inventory control, MRP
Praxa Corp. Cherry Hill, NJ	MRP and Capacity Planning Systems	Master production schedule, MRP, file maintenance, bill of material, inventory management and control, capacity planning
Professional Computer Resources, Inc. Oak Brook, IL	Resource Management System	Inventory management, MRP, production control, forecasting, capacity requirements planning

Company Name	Product Name	Modules
R.A.I.R., Inc. Mountain View, CA	MADIC	Bill of material, inventory control, work in process, requirement generation, capacity requirements planning
Rath & Strong Systems Products Lexington, MA	PIOS	Master production schedule, shop floor control, work center and routing processor, bill of material, purchase order control, MRP, order entry costing
Remote Business Services, Inc. Norwalk, CT	Manufacturing Systems for DEC System	Bill of materials, MRP, purchasing, order processing, work order preparation, scheduling inventory, sales analysis, archive (data base management system and report generator)
	Box Manufacturing System	Same as above, only specifically designed for box manufacturers
The Service Bureau Co. Div. of Control Data Greenwich, CT	MFG/PLUS	Master production schedule, inventory control, bill of material, shop floor control, purchasing, forecasting, capacity requirements planning, net change MRP, job costing

Company Name	Product Name	Modules
SESA, Inc. Boston, MA	SESAP	MRP, bill of material, shop floor control, inventory management control, master production scheduling, purchasing
Software International Andover, MA	Manufacturing Resource Planning System	Master production schedule, advanced purchasing, shop floor control, MRP, capacity requirements planning
Software Management Systems, Inc. Denver, CO	Manufacturing, Management and Control	Bill of material, master production schedule, price control, forecasting and analysis, inventory control, shop floor, tool inventory, purchaser and vendor performance, capacity requirements planning, MRP
Sperry Univac Blue Bell, PA	UNIS 1100	Production engineering data management, product costing, customer order processing, purchase order control, inventory status control, master scheduling, forecasting and analysis, material requirements planning, production planning, work order control
	UNIS 90 VS/9	Same as UNIS 1100
	UNIS 90 OS/3	Same as UNIS 1100

Company Name	**Product Name**	**Modules**
Sperry Univac (continued)	UNIS 80 MANMAN	Same as UNIS 1100 Bill of material, processing, cost accounting, work in process control, capacity planning, scheduling, materials requirements planning, inventory control, purchasing
STSC, Inc. Boston, MA	CMCS	Data base maintenance, sales forecasting, inventory management, distribution, master scheduling, MRP, capacity planning, shop floor control, stock status and order entry (highly customized)
Systemation, Inc. Cleveland, OH	MRP System	Master production schedule, engineering data control, MRP, order release
Systems Management, Inc. Des Plaines, IL	Manufacturing Control System	Bill processor and shop calendar, inventory control, on-order and master schedule, MRP, cost control, operational routing, shop floor control, capacity planning, work in process

Company Name	Product Name	Modules
Thomas, Laguban & Associates Barrington, IL	E-TAPS and E-PICS	MRP, capacity requirements planning, master production schedule, purchasing, shop floor control
Tymshare, Inc. Cupertino, CA	MANUFACTS	Inventory control, bill of material, MRP, shop floor control, master production schedule, capacity requirements planning, purchasing
U.S.S. Engineers & Consultants, Inc. (UEC) Pittsburgh, PA	Production Planning and Control System	Order entry and planning, material scheduling, warehousing
Williams & Associates San Luis Obispo, CA	IMP (Interactive Manufacturing Planning)	Materials planning, order entry, inventory control, capacity planning, requirements pegging, cost control, WIP monitor bill of material processor, purchasing
Xerox Computer Services Los Angeles, CA	Manufacturing Services	Inventory control, master production scheduling, production control, MRP, cost planning and control, capacity requirements planning, shop floor control

Data Communication Carriers

American Telephone and Telegraph Company
New York, NY

General Telephone & Electronics Corporation
Stamford, CT

Western Union Corporation
Upper Saddle River, NJ

ITT World Communications, Inc.
New York, NY

United Telecommunications, Inc.
Kansas City, MO

TRT Telecommunications, Inc.
Washington, DC

Tymnet, Inc.
Cupertino, CA

Continental Telephone Corporation
Atlanta, GA

Central Telephone & Utilities Corporation
Chicago, IL

Western Union International, Inc. (WUI)
New York, NY

Comsat Communications Satellite Corporation
Washington, DC

RCA Corporation
New York, NY

Graphic Scanning Corporation
Englewood, NJ

Southern Pacific Communications Company
Burlinglame, CA

Rochester Telephone Corporation
Rochester, NY 14646

MCI Communications Corporation
Washington, DC

American Satellite Corporation
Germantown, MD

FTC Communications
New York, NY

Computer Hardware by Vendor in Thousands of Operations Per Second

Vendor Hardware	Operations Per Second in Thousands
Amdahl	
470V/5	2,487
470V/5-11	2,850
470V/6	3,450
470V/6-11	3,750
470V/7B	3,825
470V/7A	4,250
470V/7	5,950
470V/8	6,375
Burroughs	
1750	46
1707	55
1709	60
1713	65
1830	70
1715	70
1717	75
2700	95
1776	100
3700	170
1726	175
1860	180
2830	200
1728	200
1870	200
4700	340
3830	3400

Vendor Hardware	Operations Per Second in Thousands
6807	340
6803	382
6700	425
6806	450
6805	459
6807	544
6808	545
4840	718
6810	765
6811	765
6812	765
7750	845
7803	845
7805	900
6817	1,147
6818	1,150
6821	1,260
6822	1,260
7755	1,300
7760	1,528
7770	1,950
7811	2,100
7765	2,350
7780	2,535
7775	3,000
7785	3,900
7821	4,000
Control Data Corp.	
Omega 480-1	321
171	520
Omega 480-11	553
Omega 480-111	950
72	1,000
172	1,230
73	1,300
173	1,870
74	2,500
6600	2,500
174	2,805

Vendor Hardware	**Operations Per Second in Thousands**
Control Data Corp. (continued)	
76	3,120
6700	3,700
175	5,060
176	9,360
7600	10,000
CYBER205 Vector	800,000
Cray	
1.5 Vector	800,000
Digital Equipment Corp.	
1040	165
1050KA	166
1055(2x)	307
2040	462
1060	496
1070Kl	497
PDP 11/60	510
PDP 11/70	600
1066 (2x)	600
1077 (2x)	746
1090KL	829
1080	829
2050	829
VAX-11/780	831
1099 (2x)	1,160
1088 (2x)	1,160
Honeywell	
Level 62	75
62/40B	100
64/20	100
64/20C	125
64/30	135
64/40	162
62/60D	163
64/50	219
64/DPS320	213
66/05	270
64/60	273
66/10	350

Vendor Hardware	Operations Per Second in Thousands
66/05 (2x)	405
DPS8/20	473
66/10 (2x)	525
66/07 (time-shared)	540
66/20	560
66/17 (time-shared)	700
DPS 8/44	710
66/40	900
66/20 (2x)	1,008
66/27 (time-shared)	1,120
DPS8/52	1,200
66/60	1,266
66/80	1,300
66/40 (2x)	1,620
DPS 8/70	1,987
66/60 (2x)	2,278
66/80 (2x)	2,340
DPS 8/70 (2x)	3,576
DPS 8/70 (3x)	5,007
DPS 8/70 (4x)	6,510

Note: All Honeywell numbers are based on the 66/80 performance.

IBM
System 3/32	20
360/22	36
360/30	36
260/25	40
System 3	55
370/115	55
360/40	70
370/115-2	77
370/125	80
370/125-2	99
System 3/34	110
360/50	158
370/135	161
4331	213
370/138	214
370/145	300
370/148	425
370/155	550

Vendor Hardware	**Operations Per Second in Thousands**
IBM (continued)	
360/65	568
360/75	700
4341	758
370/158	829
370/158-3	900
3031	1,045
370/165	1,900
360/85	2,100
370/168	2,300
3032	2,500
370/168-3	2,500
3033N	4,000
360/195	4,750
370/195	4,750
3033U	5,900
Magnuson	
M80/3	321
M80/31	430
M80/4	531
M80/32	531
M80/42	834
M80/43	985
Nanodata	
QMX6333	380
QMX6336	550
QMX6343	880
National Advanced Systems (Itel)	
AS/4	595
AS/5-1	829
AS/5-3	900
AS/4MP	1,000
AS/5-1MP	1,407
AS/5-3MP	1,530
AS/6	3,000
NCR	
V-8455	179
V-8555M	277

Vendor Hardware	Operations Per Second in Thousands
V-8560	281
V-8570	383
V-8565M	424
V-8555MP	531
V-8575M	576
V-8565MP	656
V-8585M	779
V-8575MP	884
V-8585MP	1,340
V-8650	2,650
V-8670	4,293
Sperry-Univac	
9200	19
9300	38
70/35 (RCA)	54
70/46 (RCA)	83
70/3 (RCA)	83
90/25	100
70/45 (RCA)	105
70/2 (RCA)	105
9400	110
9480	110
90/30	139
System 80 Mod 3	160
70/55 (RCA)	237
90/60	240
System 80 Mod 5	250
70/61 (RCA)	287
70/7 (RCA)	287
90/60E	295
70/60 (RCA)	300
70/6 (RCA)	300
90/70	329
9700	344
1100/11	392
1106	400
418-111	400
1100/60C1	544
1100/61C1	560

Vendor Hardware	**Operations Per Second in Thousands**
Sperry-Univac (continued)	
1106-11	571
90/80-2	600
1100/11 (overlap)	614
494	650
1100/61C2	672
1100/60C2	680
1108	760
90/80-3	800
90/80	825
1100/12	1,044
1100/41	1,069
90/80-4	1,100
1100/61H1	1,120
1110 (1 by 1)	1,143
1100/60H1	1,156
1108MP	1,290
1100/61H2	1,344
1100/60H2	1,496
1100/62E1	1,496
1100/62E2	1,700
1100/81	1,800
1100/42	1,918
1110 (2 by 2)	1,943
1100/62H1	2,244
1100/43	2,798
1100/62H2	2,800
1110 (4 by 4)	3,303
1100/82	3,360
1100/44	3,615
1100/83	5,040
1100/84	6,400

Report Generators by Vendor

Name	Vendor
Answer/2	Informatics, Inc.
ASI-ST	Applications Software, Inc.
CA-Earl	Computer Associates, Inc.
Culprit	Cullinane Corp.
The Data Analyzer	Program Products, Inc.
DYL-260	Dylak or Software Systems, Inc.
Easytrieve	Pansophic Systems, Inc.
Extracto	Optipro, Inc.
Mark IV	Informatics, Inc.
Quikjob III	System Support Software, Inc.
Utility-Coder	Cambridge Computer Associates, Inc.

Minicomputers by Vendor

Vendor	Computer System
Basic Four Corp.	System 600/700
Burroughs Corp.	B1900
Data General Corp.	Nova
Data General Corp.	Eclipse (16-bit)
Data General Corp.	Eclipse MV/8000 (32-bit)
Datapoint Corp.	Attached Resource Computer ARC
Datapoint Corp.	1800 Dispersed Processing System
Digital Equipment Corp.	PDP-11
Digital Equipment Corp.	VAX-11/780
Digital Equipment Corp.	VAX-11/750
Four Phase Systems, Inc.	IV/90
Harris Corp.	1600 Series
Hewlett-Packard Co.	HP 3000
IBM	Series/1
IBM	8100
Modular Computer Systems, Inc.	Classic 7800 Series
Perkin-Elmer Corp.	3200
Prime Computer, Inc.	Series 50
Systems Engineering Laboratories	32 Series (32-bit)
Tandem Computers, Inc.	T/16
Univac	System 80 (32-bit)
Univac	V77
Wang Laboratories, Inc.	VS Series 16- & 32-bit
Xerox Corp.	Diablo 3000, Systems 510

Personnel Service Organizations

Robert Half

M. David Lowe

Data Processing Careers

Fox-Morris

Data Pro

Cadillac Associates

Romac

National Personnel Consultants

Source EDP

Management Recruiters

U.S. Computer Services Companies

Control Data Corp.
Automatic Data Processing, Inc.
General Electric Information Systems
Tymshare, Inc.
United Information Systems, Inc.
McDonnell Douglas Automation Co.
Computer Sciences Corp.
NCR Corp.
Bradford National Corp.
National CSS, Inc.
Bank of America
Comshare, Inc.
Mead Data Corp.
Boeing Computer Services Co.
TRW Information Systems
University Computing Co.
Xerox Computer Services
National Data Corp.
Trans Union Systems Corp.
First Data Resources
Bunker Ramo Corp.

Index